TRANSFORMING
DARKNESS to LIGHT
for Giving

Spiritual Lessons from
My Life with a Serial Killer

Travis F. Vining

BellaRosaBooks

Transforming Darkness to Light, for Giving
ISBN 978-1-933523-47-7

First Edition: September 2011

Library of Congress Control Number: 2011937300

Printed in the United States of America on acid-free paper.

Also available in ebook form: eISBN 978-1-933523-46-0

Cover photograph by Roxanne Vining

BellaRosaBooks and logo are trademarks of Bella Rosa Books.

10   9   8   7   6   5   4   3   2   1

Table of Contents

Acknowledgments

God placed many wonderful people throughout my life to help me along the way. Some made more of an impact than others, but all helped point the way to freedom through their kindness and love.

At the most difficult time, God sent me an angel. Meeting my wife Lisa dramatically changed the course of my life. Our daughter Tori taught me the meaning of unconditional love and I was given the opportunity to experience the childhood that I thought I had missed *with her*. She has been one of my greatest teachers. My wife and daughter have brought more joy to my life than I thought possible. I am grateful for their love, friendship, support and patience.

I am also grateful to my Big Brother, JB. Sharing this journey with him has been inspiring and enlightening.

A final note to my friends and teachers, Bill Walker and Toni Furbringer.

To Toni for making me aware that I had signed up for *A Course In Miracles*.

And to Bill . . .

I am forever grateful that you dedicated your life to dealing with "those that Our Father sent you" just as Jesus did. I am grateful that I am one of them, and promise to pass it on!

> "We do not want you to become idle, but imitate those who through faith and patience inherit what was promised."
>
> —Hebrews 6:11-12

Introduction

My father is a serial killer. I was his confidante as he planned and committed several murders. He enjoyed telling me about them. He also used me to help destroy evidence.

I am responsible for solving three of the murders seventeen years after they happened. It became unbearable to keep our little secret. In fact, it was killing me. Now it's my dad that wants to kill to me. He has described in his letters to me from Death Row just how obsessed he is with murdering his once favorite son.

I didn't believe that it was possible to makes sense of all of this. I was wrong. Everything that happens to us in our lives can be explained, understood and *forgiven*. It is not always easy and requires great faith and courage, but it is promised to all of us.

This is a true story about a father and his son. It is about a journey through hell that led to heaven. It is about faith, miracles, courage, forgiveness and overcoming tragedy. It is about the freedom that can always be found in our darkest moments. It is about how to get *there* . . . from *here.*

It is an extraordinary journey to go from wanting nothing more than your own father's approval in life to accepting his intense hatred and threats without any feelings of regret or sadness. But true *forgiveness* is extremely powerful.

This *forgiveness* led me to my real Father, the one who has all power. I know this to be true because God's love is all over this story. God was always there. I simply needed to learn how to recognize his presence and accept his grace.

Is it possible to make sense of what we perceive as tragic

and unforgivable events in our lives? What could murder, pain, suffering and insanity possibly have to do with peace, freedom and a loving God? And the even bigger, more personal question that many of us ask ourselves when tragedy strikes our lives, is *why me*? The answers to these questions may surprise you. I went through hell to find them, and for that,

I Am Forever Grateful.
I Am Forgiven.

Chapter 1

Revealing a Killer's Secrets

Tuesday, January 5, 2010

I started my day the same way I had started every other day for the past few years. I woke up, thanked God for this day and began to quiet my mind for meditation. This particular morning was going to require a little extra effort. I was headed out to a place that held some of my fondest memories of my dad. It was the place that I felt most connected to him as a young teenager. It was where we hunted, laughed and camped together. It is also where he buried his friend that he murdered, another experience that bonded us together.

It was four-thirty A.M. I sat comfortably on our living room floor as the moonlight came streaming through our French Doors. It was our formal living room and we didn't have any furniture in it. I sat facing the moon as I quieted my mind. After this quiet time I ended with a few simple prayers, mostly about healing for my family and friends. My last thought before getting up was a hopeful prayer that whatever was to happen today would bring healing to others and that I would recognize my role in it. I felt peaceful as I finished with the sign of the cross. It was time to go.

This morning was also a hunting trip that involved my father. We were hunting for a body. The body of my father's long time friend and associate that he had murdered twenty-two years earlier. It was my father's first victim. It was also the murder that revealed to me for the first time exactly who and what my father was all those years ago. Not that I accepted it at the time.

He told me about his plan to kill his friend just before it happened. That was the murder that started it all. Now, it was about to end right where it all began. It was time to close this wound.

It was an unusually cold January morning in Central Florida. In fact, it was one of the coldest weeks on record with temperatures in the high twenties and low thirties. It had also rained a great deal and there was a lot of water on the ground. I knew this was going to be a problem when looking for the body of my father's friend, but we went anyway.

A couple of weeks earlier I had finally received what I had been hoping for. My dad sent me a written confession detailing exactly how and where he killed his friend. It was not easy getting this. It also revealed some very ugly truths about my father that were hard to process, but extremely important for me to see.

To get him to confess I used the only leverage that I had with my father . . . money. I had mailed him money on Death Row for years and he had become very accustomed to having his snacks, television, reading materials, and most importantly, cigarettes. He had become too comfortable, in part, because taking these things away from him after twenty years on Death Row suddenly made being there intolerable for him. These extras were his only source of comfort and he had come to absolutely rely upon them.

My father was sentenced to death for the murder of a diamond dealer in Orlando, Florida in 1990, and although he was the suspect in three other slayings at the time, he would get away with them for fourteen years—until I came forward in 2004 to help cold case detectives solve them. That is where justice began to enter the picture. Five years later, this is where it seemed to be coming to a close.

When I began to put pressure on my dad by taking away his money, I was already responsible for his being convicted of two other murders. A few years earlier I had a life changing experience that brought back the memories of the time that I spent with my father, as his trusted confidante, when he was murdering people. I had traveled to Death Row and recorded a conversation with him. He had unknowingly confessed to these two murders, but I had been unable to get him to talk about his friend's murder . . . until now.

Taking the prison comforts away from him whipped him into a frenzy that revealed to me just how dangerous my father still is. It opened a window into the mind of a sociopathic killer. My father wrote letters threatening to kill me and my family. These letters included details about what he fantasized about doing to me and my family. It was the vilest material that I have ever read, and it was directed at me, from my dad. It was hard to absorb at first, but then I began to see the beauty of it all.

What I saw reminded me of just how lucky I was to be alive today. It also explained a lot about why I did, or didn't do, certain things all those years ago when my father was killing people.

I was thinking about all of this as I drove towards the Deseret Ranch in Holopaw, Florida. It's a cattle ranch in the center of the state that includes tens of thousands of acres of beautiful pastures and woods. It was still dark and the drive there was about forty-five minutes. On the way, I began to reflect back on this whole journey. There was so much to think about, it was hard to get my mind around it.

I would go from remembering what it felt like to be around him while he was committing these crimes to trying to understand his intense hatred for me now. That would lead me to think about the miracles that I had witnessed over the past few years, then back to my father again. It has been like this for me for years. I have a tendency to separate the miracles from the murders and experience them with completely different emotions.

It's not easy to understand and to accept that they are

connected and belong together, but they are. One cannot be separated from the other. Here in lies one of the problems in life that creates separation in so many of us. This separation is based on a very limited understanding of the world around us and that causes us to live with so much unnecessary fear. The removal of that fear takes work, courage, pain and faith. When it begins to become clear, and the seemingly senseless acts of suffering suddenly make sense, an incredible feeling of peace replaces that fear.

I kept reminding myself of this fact as I remembered all the events that led up to this morning. Mostly, I was remembering the heavy stuff . . . the murders and what it felt like to be around my father before and after he killed these people. There was still an attraction to that feeling, as sick as it was. Although I am beginning to really see the beauty in all this, I am not yet able to stay in that peace without interruption.

My thoughts were bouncing around a bit from crime to crime. It was still hard to put it all in some sort of nice and neat order. My dad killed four people and I was with him either before or immediately following all of these crimes. I now can remember vividly his behavior, his mannerisms. That's what I remember the most, his behavior.

The guy we were looking for was his first murder. As I drove I thought about how it all started. We were in his car, driving down a beautiful country road in Apopka, Florida, when I asked my dad a question that would solidify my part in this. He was baiting me, I know that now. He wanted me to ask. He wanted to tell someone what he was going to do. What he was capable of. He really wanted to share this, and as his son, I accepted the role of confidante.

He didn't give me any details, just that he had a land deal with his friend that would make him rich. I didn't understand, so he explained it to me. His friend's two million dollar piece of property in the Keys was about to be deeded to him in an imaginary land deal. The question that I asked, the one he was waiting for, hoping for . . . was simple. *Why would he let that happen, couldn't he stop it after he learned that there were no buyers?* His answer was just as simple and very clear. My dad looked at me as he studied my behavior and said, "He won't be around to dispute the deal." That cemented our relationship for the next seventeen months. I was now a part of this, and as much as I tried to deny it, I knew it. It made me sick, but I couldn't show it.

For me, the most disturbing and confusing part of all this was being in the presence of your worst nightmare while still hoping that you can go to the very same source for protection from it. The feeling inside was total chaos, as if I were being drawn to, and pulled from, something at the same time . . . stuck with no apparent way out. I was reliving that experience as I came closer and closer to our old hunting camp.

As I became more familiar with the area approaching the ranch, I began to drift off into memories of better days, hunting and fishing with my dad. I thought of him laughing, us drinking together and telling stories. Mostly how wonderful life was and how the whole world was in front of me. I so loved my dad and this was the place that we were closest. It was during these hunting trips that I felt closest to my dad. A father, as it turned out, that I never really knew.

The emotional swings brought me to tears. I was listening to a song in my CD player that was all about the feelings that I was having. No coincidence, it was exactly what I needed to hear. The crying was pretty heavy, but it felt good. It didn't last long but there was an odd sort of closeness with my father involved in it. It was as if we were becoming closer than ever before. Maybe it's because the secrets were gone. I didn't resent what he had done any more. All these emotions were mixed in together, but it felt good, cleansing.

I was beginning to understand just how connected he and I really were, and still are. I felt like everything was exactly as it was supposed to be. Making sense of these horrible crimes never seemed possible, but that is exactly what was happening. The power of forgiveness was shining a welcome light on the dark past, turning these once shadowy figures into beautiful spiritual lessons of peace.

As my emotions went back and forth, the underlying feelings were gratitude, peace and anticipation. That may not make sense, but that is how I felt. I was getting much better at remembering those old feelings while staying grounded in peace. The key was that I wasn't afraid to *go there* anymore. It would continue to get easier still.

As I came closer I began to focus more on all the miracles that I had witnessed since I re-opened this old wound and allowed it to begin to heal. As I approached the entrance to the Ranch the peace of it all settled back over me. Thank God for *coincidences*.

When I pulled up a couple of big four-wheel drive trucks, along with some unmarked police cars, were waiting for me. It was kind of exciting. I really liked being around these guys because they were here to help me solve this. Many of my friends didn't understand what I was doing, and it was difficult to explain, but when it came to the crime aspect of this, these guys were all ears. They were interested, and they had experience with it. I liked the way it made me feel.

One of the trucks had the cadaver dogs in the back. There were two of them. We exchanged some pleasantries, talked a little about what we were going to do and started heading down a long dirt road towards the entrance to the ranch. This place was, and still is, beautiful. It is a part of Florida that many people never get to see. I had spent a lot of time here, camping and hunting with my dad, and now I was being flooded with a whole new set of memories and feelings.

After about a mile, on this heavily graded dirt road, surrounded by mostly brush and thick woods, we turned onto what we used to call the "yellow brick road." It is an old brick road that used to run across the state connecting Melbourne to Tampa. This is the only section of it that I have ever seen. It runs through some beautiful oak trees and wooded areas before opening up into endless pastures, wetlands and woods.

It's like entering paradise through a nature-covered driveway that connects two very different worlds. It felt good to be back here.

As we drove the property, I paid very close attention the roads. My father's confession of the crimes detailed where he buried his friend, stating that he used the Cadillac to get there. If his story was to work, the place we were headed had to be accessible by a car. So far, his story was checking out, but now we were about to enter the property through a locked gate, and according to the aerial map my father gave me, we had a couple of more miles to go into the woods before coming to the area that he had circled on the map.

When I was a kid, the gate was where I left all the cares of the outside world behind. We didn't have cell phones back then, so when we entered the property, we were cut off from the outside world for days at a time. I was reminded of that feeling as we drove through the gate.

It was strange, after all these years, coming back to this place of sacred memories with my dad, accompanied by homicide detectives, trucks and dogs. Like everything else, it was all mixed up together now. I couldn't help but think that he wasn't who I thought he was back then either, but man did I love him. Then, I wanted to be just like him, or so I thought.

The best he ever treated me was when we were here. It wasn't the hunting that made this fun; it was sitting around the campfire, drinking and telling stories with my dad, my friend and uncle. Laughing is what we did the most. It's strange to think about now. It seemed so real, but nothing was as it seemed.

There is a great deal of pasture land on this ranch, and it's very open. We were studying the aerial map from my father as we looked at the satellite images in the truck. The ranch includes thousands of acres, and it was hard to be sure from the ground if we were headed to the right spot. It was not far from the natural main road, just on the edge of a wooded area.

The first place we stopped seemed to match, but something kept bothering me about it. There was a feed plot for deer, just like in the photo, but it was positioned differently on the map than on the ground. We began to search and they let the dogs out. I watched for awhile, hoping for something, but they seemed to be getting nowhere. As they were searching, I wandered off into the woods.

This was near a place that we once camped, and I wanted to find that place. I am not sure why, but I am drawn to places where heavy, important, and emotional events happened in my life, and this was certainly one of them. It seems these places still hold some of that emotion in the air, almost like its part of the history, still there. I don't know if others feel that way, but I definitely have a much deeper experience of an event if I am where it actually took place.

As I walked through the woods approaching our old campsite, I could feel the anticipation. It was a happy place, and it still felt that way. The site was still recognizable, and I stood there for a while, taking it all in. I completely forgot about why I was there, just enjoying the site.

After a few minutes, when I realized they might be looking for me, I decided to go back, but it wasn't easy to leave. Once again, it was time to cross over from one reality to another. It still felt like I was going between two worlds. Well, actually three. This third world that I was experiencing was bringing the other two together, revealing a much bigger truth for me, a revelation that would explain so much of the unexplainable.

When I returned to where they were, the police investigators were getting discouraged. It was cold, and there was a lot of water on the ground that made it difficult to use the dogs. I finally said something about the feed plot. They didn't seem to think it was a big deal until one of the guys found another spot on the satellite close by that matched the description better, so we moved.

I jumped in the truck with the guy who decided to take another look, and we went on ahead while they cleaned up and rested the dogs. As we approached this new spot, I noticed that the road was easily accessible by car, all the way to the edge of the woods. The other spot was harder to reach, and that bothered me as well. Now we were on to something, and the detective knew it, too.

Something inside was telling me this was it. It did match everything on the map, but that wasn't it, it was much deeper than that. My disappointment was being replaced with a sense of optimism and maybe even closure. I am not a big fan of using the word closure, but that is the only way to describe what I was feeling. I felt that I was getting close, and that excited me.

This was also near another spot where we once camped, also described in his letter, and it all matched. The other detectives would join us after we walked the area for a while, but the dogs were cold and tired by now. They only spent a few minutes on the area before deciding to come back when the conditions were better and some of the water was gone.

There was an area that my father described in his letter as a pond bog, surrounded by trees with a lone cypress tree on the corner of it. I was standing on that very spot. He wrote that the pond was dry when he buried his friend on May 31, 1987, but that it held water in the rainy season. This day, after all the rain we had, it was full of water, but you could tell it was temporary, just like in his letter.

As I stood there, I knew this part of the journey was over. I was done trying to make right the past by solving these old murders. I ran from this trouble for years, and now it was all out there for everyone to see. I wasn't keeping my father's secrets anymore. These same secrets had almost killed me, but were now giving me back my freedom.

One of the detectives asked how I felt about all this. I simply said, "I'm done with this. I will not be coming back out here. I know all I need to know and did all I needed to do."

It's funny how if you really want to leave something like this behind, you have to go back through it before you can let it go. The reason for this seems to be more of a fact-finding mission than simply reliving the past. It was for me anyway.

To let go of the past, I began to go back through the years to find out the truth about my dad. At least that's what I thought I was doing. This fact-finding mission revealed some truths about me too, and as it turned out, those were the ones that I needed to find the most. I had a lot of my father in me. The more I learned about him, the more I wanted it out of me . . . all of it.

I had to look really hard to find the truth and it wasn't easy. My father wasn't the only one keeping secrets from me. I had become quite good at it myself.

Chapter 2

Painmaker—Raised by a Sociopath

My father appeared to be a very successful business man. I had an older brother and sister from his marriage to my mom and a younger half-brother and half-sister from his second marriage to my stepmother. Our family lived in a home on Biscayne Bay, had money and was very well known. My father had three brothers, all successful and well connected in Miami and South Florida. He served as a pilot in the Air Force, was very good looking and extremely charming. From the outside, our life looked almost perfect.

Like any young boy, I idolized my dad. When in his presence, I was almost hypnotized by him. I was extremely attracted to the way he approached life. I guess it's normal for a boy to want to be just like his father. I wanted to believe everything that he told me. As best I could tell, he treated me pretty well. He took care of me, gave me money, taught me to hunt and spent time teaching me lessons about life.

Unfortunately, these lessons were coming from a different perspective on life than most children are exposed to, from that of a sociopath. A sociopath is a person who operates without conscience or remorse and is incapable of love. For the most part, sociopaths treat their children like possessions, and I was my father's favorite. He treated me special and I liked it. All of this only added to my confusion as a kid, because much of the time he seemed like a great dad. Still, something wasn't right. There were conditions attached to his love, and I knew it. This underlying uneasiness was causing me problems, too.

From as far back as I can remember I would have terrifying recurring nightmares. I didn't understand why and didn't talk about it because I thought it was a sign of weakness. I would wake up in the middle of the night, gasping for breath and feel as if the weight of the world was crushing down on me. I couldn't breathe, and would feel a serious and frightening threat that I didn't understand. This threat was extremely elusive and I couldn't identify what it was. I didn't know where the threat was coming from, only that it was close. It was always close, surrounding me on all sides. The dreams felt real. I tried to dismiss them as just "kid stuff", but I was really scared. I hated myself for this.

I always felt unsettled and frightened. Something just wasn't right, and I couldn't quite put my finger on it. It might have been just a small detail, but it felt really important. My mind would tell me that it just didn't add up or make sense. With no point of reference, the only thing I knew to do was to let it go. Whatever the conflict, I was not able to reconcile the problem or rationalize what it meant to me. Consequently, I would bury it. What I was seeing was so frightening that I didn't want to know the truth. A lie was more acceptable. I lived in this confusing space.

On the outside I probably appeared to be like any other kid my age. I made good grades, was fairly outgoing, had friends and tried my best to fit in. It helped that I always had nice things and could afford to do most anything that my friends did. My dad taught me to be respectful and to say *yes sir* and *no sir* when addressing adults. They liked that, and I was typically a favorite of my friends' parents.

The problem was that while my father was teaching me some of the right ideas his behavior was offering a different point of view. This was my experience with my father, and it happened often. His behavior was raising questions that I could not answer. I can see them now, but at the time, I didn't want to believe what I was seeing or feeling. I would try to redirect my attention to something else that would make that feeling go away.

Looking back, there were so many signs that it's almost impossible to believe that we didn't know that my father was *different*. When I say we, I am referring to my entire family. This is the most mystifying part of this. How we are able to deny these things is still an incredibly baffling and dangerous characteristic of human nature.

With my father, all of the signs were there. It's not that they were hidden all that well. The signs were out in the open for all to observe, yet we could not accept the truth about Dad. I think it was a combination of his charm and our unwillingness to accept that someone we know and love could be like this. More importantly, I think, was our inability to understand how this could even be possible. That's the main blocker. We have no way of identifying with another person's ability to operate without conscience. It's so foreign that we don't recognize it.

For family it's even more difficult. In my case, I had nothing to compare it to. For me, it was just Dad. Not only could I not identify the characteristics, but I wanted to be like him. This tells me that we did see the characteristics, but didn't process them properly. This led to all kinds of problems for me. I somehow developed a conscience, thank God, but that made it impossible for me to live up to my father's image. This was an insurmountable dilemma for me. I never could put my finger on what I was trying to become and why I couldn't get there.

For starters, nobody really knew for sure what Dad did for a living. He could not explain it properly, but he didn't seem to care. It was hidden for years by the fact that he was a real estate broker, but after several questionable land deals he lost his license. After that he simply said he was an investor without giving any more detail.

He also didn't seem to have any lifelong friends to speak of. All were temporary and most left after being caught up in some sort of scam, whether it was buying a boat with my father, or investing in land with him. They all got taken at some point. He used everyone, including family. This was the one constant in his life.

His relationships were not healthy. He literally destroyed my mom in a divorce when I was only four, and he received custody of us three kids. She got nothing and left the marriage with her life in complete shambles. He then married a woman thirteen years younger, a woman who had no business raising children. She despised us kids but did a pretty good job of hiding it from others in the family. They either ignored what signs were there or didn't want to get involved. When we tried to tell them, they explained it away and simply dismissed us as just unhappy kids. My dad wasn't the least bit concerned about how my stepmother abused us; it was up to us to take care of ourselves.

I certainly didn't know it at the time, but I was developing deep-rooted and serious trust issues with adults, especially as it related to my own family. This was confirming my worst fears. Everywhere I turned for help, I was questioned about my own motives and truthfulness. It always came back to my credibility and no one seemed to take me or my siblings seriously. When things on the outside began to look questionable, everyone seemed to dismiss it. This only added to the insanity of it all for me.

Dad was beginning to get tangled up in all kinds of lawsuits, and the newspaper started to take notice. In the early seventies *The Miami News* did a series of articles about a land deal that my father orchestrated, calling it "Secret Land Trusts". Someone made hundreds of thousands of dollars, and the newspaper implied that it was my dad. It seemed that everyone my father knew was caught up in this scheme. His banker, political friends, business associates and even his secretary were all named in this so-called mysterious land deal.

There were other signs of my father's dark nature. He was a self-proclaimed racist and he hated women. He was very vocal about this and did not hide his feelings. In fact, he was proud of his position of superiority and judgment of others. Women were simply inferior beings with but one purpose. He spoke of them as a necessary evil. He often said that women would have a bounty on their head if not for sex (to put it mildly). The strange part, even at this early age, was that I knew he meant it literally.

One of the most disturbing signs that everyone dismissed was my father's fascination for Hitler. He didn't just collect Third Reich memorabilia; my father admired Hitler and thought he should have done more. This was out in the open with our family. He had a Nazi flag that covered the entire ceiling of his den upstairs, along with SS knives, guns, and other Nazi collectables from the war.

My father listened to tapes of Hitler's speeches from the war. Sometimes when he came home from work drunk, he asked me to sit in the car with him to listen to these tapes. As a young boy, this was my quality time with dad. I loved it when he was drunk because he showed more affection and seemed more interested in spending time together. I didn't think much about the subject matter, I was just happy that he wanted to spend time with me. I didn't know that what he was teaching me was pure hatred because I didn't have any other trusted point of reference. Sometimes, however, I intuitively knew just how wrong it was.

At one point we lived in a million-dollar home on Biscayne Bay in an exclusive community in Coral Gables. Our Jewish neighbors were constantly bothering him, and one Sunday he played Nazi records of these Hitler speeches all day from our garage facing their house. He laughed as he told me how they were worthless pieces of humanity that should have been exterminated.

The scariest part of all of this was that, depending on the circumstances, he seemed to be able to direct these same feelings towards his own family. At my stepmother's request he sent my older brother and sister away to boarding school, basically kicking them out of the house at a very young age. He said they were both screw-ups and didn't deserve to live at home anymore. His tone sounded frighteningly familiar.

Our family was a train wreck, but nobody seemed to notice. We just kept on going. For us kids, it was our normal. We didn't know any better. There didn't seem to be anywhere to turn for help.

I love my mother dearly, but she couldn't give us what we needed, either. She was an alcoholic and never fully recovered from the divorce. She was absolutely devastated from losing us kids to my father. He ruined her in court with false testimony and witnesses. It was a complete character assassination for all to see. He was ruthless, to say the least, and now she had experienced what it felt like to be on the wrong side of this man.

She struggled to survive and did the best she could, but she was heartbroken. When I was twelve years old, she called me one night very drunk and told me goodbye. It took me a while to figure out what she was doing because she was slurring her words so badly, but I came to realize that she was committing suicide.

I went to my father and begged him to take me to her. He didn't want to be bothered. I was crying hysterically and he finally agreed to take me to her apartment. Once we were there he refused to get out of the car. The whole scene disgusted him. I banged on the door, but she did not answer. After several attempts I took a small towel from my father's car, wrapped it around my fist and broke the jalousie windows in her door to enter her apartment. She was barely awake and heavily drugged from a combination of Valium and alcohol. I called 9-1-1, and the police sent an ambulance.

As sick as this was, the most disturbing part of that night was my father's behavior. Hers made sense to me. His did not. He simply didn't care. At the time I rationalized that it was because he didn't love my mom and he was just a tough guy. I looked up to my dad because he was so *tough*. He had always taught me that being tough was an important quality for successful men, but this wasn't right. My mom was trying to kill herself and he didn't bother to get out of the car to help, and when I asked him for help, he showed little or no emotion. It wasn't his problem. He would have been okay if she had died that night right in front of me. In fact, he wanted it. That is what I felt, but I got busy burying that thought.

That *something's not right here* feeling or thought was then replaced by how he reacted to me. I also didn't like the thought of my father's being so cold that he could watch me deal with that alone and not care what it was doing to me. I guess I tried to rationalize that thought and couldn't make sense of it, so I went back to the "tough guy" explanation and tried to dismiss it. Really, if I connected the dots, the truth was not an explanation I was ready to accept at that time. I already had my hands full with circumstances that I didn't know how to deal with, and wasn't getting any help my father.

One of the many questions that I dismissed that night was why didn't Dad help me and why didn't he understand how difficult this was for me? Why didn't he hold me and tell me that it would be okay? I was extremely scared and confused. Either he really didn't care or he couldn't relate to what I was feeling. I needed him badly then, and he was suddenly completely alien to me.

Because I didn't like the answers, I dismissed the questions and tried to believe that I misunderstood his behavior. I would go as far as to begin to remember events like this differently, and blamed myself for having these weird thoughts.

The truth was that my father didn't care because he was not capable of relating to the feelings I was having. As a sociopath, he was incapable of feeling what I was feeling. He did have the ability to mimic these behaviors when he felt necessary, but he rarely bothered when he was mad, and that night he was mad.

Looking back, I can see that was a very dark and lonely night for me. I was in the presence of both my parents, but deep down I knew how alone I really was. No, I wasn't ready for the truth. It was easier to believe that I had misunderstood my dad's behavior, that everything would be okay. Dad loved me, he was just angry and everything will be fine, I told myself.

Well, everything didn't turn out fine. My dad was a con-man who would turn to murder as a serial killer later in life. This night was one glimpse of his sickness, but there were many other experiences like this one. I continued to dismiss them because they didn't make any sense to me. I may have sensed the truth, but either I could not, or was not capable of dealing with it. I think that is what was happening to me, and it kept me awake at night, gasping for air. I was having nightmares about the boogeyman alright, but this feeling of an immediate threat was not a dream. It was so real that sometimes I had a hard time separating the dream from reality.

One night I was asleep in my room when my stepmother came bursting though the door and turned on the light. It sounded like a freight train was crashing through my room. She immediately began screaming at me at the top of her lungs. I sat up in my bed terrified, disoriented and thinking this was just another nightmare. I didn't remember doing anything wrong and was sound asleep when this started.

She was yelling at me uncontrollably, telling me what a terrible kid I was. She said that she was finally sending me off to boarding school like my brother and sister. All of her problems would then be solved, she said. She'd had it with me, and I was gone. She was overflowing with venom, and I of course believed her. I was fearful that she was going to attack me physically and I froze, too paralyzed by fear to make a sound.

Suddenly, my father burst through the door behind her and physically took her down to the ground. It was all happening so fast. I was still trying to determine exactly what I did to start all this. I now knew it wasn't a dream and that was not a good feeling. This was real, and it was intense. I was terrified and disoriented. I preferred my nightmares. They were safer.

My father sat on top of my stepmother and held her down. He began to hit her in the back of the head with his forearm and told her to apologize to me. He pressed her face into the carpet with a great deal of force. Now he was the one yelling. I knew he had her and that felt good. Somehow this felt safe, and I was happy my dad was there to protect me. He was in charge now and protecting me, I thought.

As he held her down, he continued to punish her and told her again to apologize to me. I don't remember if she did, but I know she gave into him, at least to some degree. How this all ended is still fuzzy, but I remember them going back into the main part of the house and turning off the light in my room. That was it. No big deal for them. It was like it never happened. For me, my heart kept pounding uncontrollably in my chest. I kept searching my mind, frantically trying to figure out what I did to start all of this trouble.

Everything about this was all wrong, and again everything came back to my father. Although I felt like he was defending me, the fact was that he was more interested in making her pay than in consoling me. It was always like that, now that I think about it. He only protected us kids when it was convenient for him and he wanted to make a point with her. Deep down I knew that, and it didn't sit well with me. I wanted to believe that this was a good thing, but most of the time he just didn't care. I did enjoy him beating her at the time. I wanted her to feel the pain I was feeling. I wanted her to know what it felt like to feel helpless. These were not healthy thoughts, but it's how I remember feeling.

I don't recall my dad bringing it up after that night or explaining it to me. Once again, I had to play tough guy and pretend I could handle it. Around my dad I would act fine with it. That made him proud.

My dad never acted like any of this was unusual or wrong. This is all sociopath here. No conscience, no guilt . . . no compassion. He couldn't connect with what I was feeling because he didn't have those feelings.

On the other hand, I was all about guilt and conscience. As a kid, I always felt like this was part of growing up, and it was my job to learn how to handle these events and to be a better man—to be a tough guy like my dad. I thought my father didn't talk to me about these experiences because they were just part of life. And I was convinced that I was failing at this life, miserably.

There were times when my dad paid a lot of attention to us kids and I loved it. He would take us to the Monkey Jungle in South Florida on the weekends and wrestle with us in the house. We always had small farm animals of some kind around, and we would watch sports together. He also had a sense of humor and could make you laugh until you couldn't stop crying. I couldn't seem to get enough of that time with him. It was during these times that everything seemed perfect. I would get lost in the feelings that came from being close to my dad, especially when he laughed. I lived for those moments. They never lasted long, but apparently it was just enough to keep us all from seeing the real truth.

As with me, this illusion kept others in the family from putting together the pieces of the puzzle. They were holding pieces separate so they would not have to see the whole picture. I mean, if you put it all together, what would you do about it? Could you imagine realizing that your brother is a sociopath? What do you do with the kids? Do you get involved? How do you even begin to approach this problem? There were so many questions, but without a solution and nothing to compare it to, we simply choose not to put all the pieces of the puzzle together.

Today's society is filled with families who struggle with the same questions. The fears and confusion do not go away: they continue to fester. Undiagnosed and untreated, it continues to get worse. We are allowing the enemy to hide among us and wreak havoc in our lives. The victims are keeping the victimizers' secrets for them.

Failure to look more closely results is some terrifying experiences. So terrifying, in fact, that sometimes we choose not to give them a second *thought.*

Chapter 3

Too Scary to Recall—Shattered Dreams

As a young adult, I had convinced myself that my father was a successful *investor*. At least that's what I kept telling myself. He made a great deal of money, we lived in expensive homes and he always had plenty of cash.

In my early twenties, however, things suddenly changed. In 1982 we started to have money problems, serious money problems. I was twenty-two and in college at the time, or as I like to say now, pretending to go to college. My father was finding it difficult to send my monthly allowance, and this was very alarming to me. I didn't realize it, but our entire relationship was based on this money, and doing without it was unnerving as hell. It was the one thing I thought that I could count on with my dad, but I was wrong. This illusion was about to be shattered—and along with it, my entire belief system.

In the absence of my dad's most powerful weapon, the curtain was about to be pulled back, and what I was about to see was so frightening that I would literally refuse to accept it. In order to do this successfully, apparently, I would need to delete entire events from my memory. The events that I remembered, I would need to keep separate from each other. It was like having all the pieces of the puzzle, but purposely separating them so I could not see the entire picture. For insurance, I removed some of the pieces altogether. All this was happening without me being aware that I was doing it.

It was December of 1982, and I was enrolled at the

University of Florida. I was really struggling with my grades. I was drinking too much and would often black out, but I was also having fun. I had joined a fraternity, made some new friends and absolutely loved football season. I liked the freedom that came with college, but I couldn't seem to stay out of trouble. I wrecked my cars, moved a lot and was always out of money. I was living with that *I just can't seem to fit in* feeling and it was really beginning to nag at me. Then suddenly my dad dropped a bombshell on me.

He was having trouble with money and he said I needed to come home to wait until his next deal came through. Money was the only thing that I seemed to be able to rely upon with my father and suddenly that was gone. I was already living with a lot of fear, but the events of the next few short months were going to make that fear look like child's play. I really didn't know what fear was, and that was unfortunate, because I was scared.

My father began to tell me that the FBI was looking for him because of something that he did not do. He said that they had the wrong guy and that he would sue them for this when it was all over. I wanted to believe that, but I had begun to see signs of his business dealings before this, and now they were becoming increasingly more difficult to deny. The pattern was there, but I didn't want to look. I really didn't have any faith in God, and my father was my "higher power". Everything that I believed in for my existence was wrapped up in this man. This was not a good feeling so I tried not to look too closely, and I focused on his charm and promises instead.

First, my father began to reveal to me his new plan to make money, but he was very clear that he wanted me to stay away from it to "keep me clean". He justified this new plan by saying that the FBI might get him. He could wind up spending a short period of time in minimum security prison, and he had to do this for the family. It was the only way to do something fast.

What was it that my "investor father" had in mind? He

planned to start a marijuana farm in Plymouth, Florida. This was a little tough to rationalize, considering the other evidence on the table. Still, as always, my father did a good job of selling me on the idea and justifying why he had to do this . . . for us, of course. My brother was brought down from Alabama, and my father bought a chicken farm in a rural area near Apopka, Florida. We would proceed to bury a semi-tractor trailer in the ground to grow pot with hydroponics systems.

He failed to keep his promise that I would be kept out of it, but as usual, he was very clever in how he hooked me. He kept saying that he wanted to keep me clean, but he didn't mean it. It was just part of the con. He then began to share with me the trouble that he was having with my brother and all kinds of issues that he was worried about. So I *volunteered* to help. I knew it would make Dad proud and it did! He was very excited to have my help, but he continued to point out (while he was praising me) how it was my decision, and my decision only. He may have said it was mine, but it was the one he wanted and I was an easy mark. No match for the master.

My head was spinning and I recognized this familiar feeling. Everything was moving in fast motion, and I was unable to comprehend the gravity of the situation. It was just too much, and I kept relying upon Dad even more.

When I came back to Orlando my stepmother would not allow me to live in the million-dollar home that we had in a gated community. My dad set up an office in Mount Dora with a back room where I could live. The perfect set up he said; "Better for you than staying at the house because you can come and go." The only problem with this "good" living situation was that the building was rat infested, had no shower, and was attached to an already condemned building. He tried to make it look nice with paint and carpet, but the rats stayed.

I felt trapped with nowhere to go and nowhere to turn. Now, even in the evening, I was on pins and needles. After the days with my father I would break into the condemned building next to our office where I could shower. I had to work my way through falling down walls to get to it, and of course, it didn't have hot water, but my father was proud of me for roughing it out for him. After my chilling shower I would lie on my water bed and watch the rats run on the exposed pipe directly above my bed. They were large, loud and unafraid of me.

What was happening to my world? It was slipping away . . . no, not slipping away, but being yanked out from underneath me. It was as though my entire life was built on top of a huge trap door, and I didn't know it. Suddenly, that door was opening, and beneath it was an unknown hell that I didn't know existed. Everything I thought, everything that I believed, was being flushed before my very eyes, and I could not stop it or wish it away.

Next, FBI agents began showing up at the house looking for Dad. My father was in trouble, but he still kept telling us kids it would be all right. The Feds were after him, he said, but he would beat them. "They had the wrong guy," was his standard response when something went wrong, only this time, something was terribly, terribly wrong.

These guys were after my dad, and they didn't think he was so charming. One night when we were headed to the house from Mount Dora, I was driving. My father had a house in the exclusive neighborhood of Sweetwater Club in Sweetwater, Florida. Once we pulled in the gated community, a car started to follow us and my dad asked me to turn left instead of right to see if they were indeed after us. I don't know what I knew at the time . . . only that my dad had serious trouble, but I was not expecting this.

My dad changed his behavior, and he was angry. The law enforcement agents tried to pull us over while my dad told me to keep driving, and he wasn't kidding around. This scared the hell out of me. Here was an undercover agent pulling me over, and my father telling me to keep going. The agent pulled in front of the car, and my dad said to keep going forward and around his car. The cop was directly in front of me, yelling "stop", with his hand on his gun. It's hard to describe how intense this was for me. I was panicking, and I chose to stop. I was scared and knew it was the right thing to do. My father was disappointed, and he let me know it. I felt that it was my fault he was going to jail that night. Once again I proved to him (and myself) that I wasn't man enough to be like him, or at least that's what I thought. He was pissed and gave me a look that was very chilling, one that was usually reserved for the bad guys, as he liked to say.

The cops had a warrant from Alabama for my father's arrest, and they handcuffed him and put him in the car. This was another one of those moments when I didn't know how to react. I felt that they were doing the right thing, but he was my dad, my provider, and I didn't understand what this all meant to me. I felt safer with him in custody, but I wanted Dad back. These emotions didn't make sense together. I was scared and confused. Fear was everywhere I turned because that's all I knew, everything else was evaporating.

As the FBI continued to come for my father with warrants from different states, he was still maintaining his optimism. One evening I was at the house with him when agents showed up again, and he gave some instructions on how to respond. He said his lawyer was supposed to handle this and that they should not be taking him to jail every time a warrant appeared. He told me that he was going slip out the back and I was to get the door. He said not to let them in to allow him some time to sneak out the back door into the woods behind the house. He said that they could not arrest me for stalling, as it was within my legal rights, so be tough and just do it.

I answered the door and said my dad wasn't home. They had seen him drive into the neighborhood. They showed me a warrant. I did as my father said and tried to hold the door as they pushed on it. They entered the house, but he was gone. They proceeded to arrest me and charged me with resisting an officer without violence. Good old Dad got away, but I was headed to jail.

I'd never been to jail before, and I cannot recall all the emotions that I was feeling on the way to jail that night. This was a nightmare alright, but it was real, too real for me. I do remember that night once I was booked. At the time, it was the longest night of my life: the hours passed so slowly that it made me physically sick to my stomach. At first I was convinced that my stepmother would come bail me out, but as the night dragged on, it became painfully clear to me that everyone had abandoned me. This was an indescribably lonely feeling, and I had nowhere to hide from my thoughts. This was one long night. I remember trying to sleep, only to jerk straight up panicked and breathless every time I came close to sleep. The overriding questions were: what the hell is happening, where did my life go, and what am I doing in jail?

The next morning my stepmother showed up, and the court released me into her custody. When I hooked up with my father that day he was *proud* of me for what I did. I was now really earning his respect, he said. "This is good and we are going to sue those bastards for a million dollars . . . This is good" he said again. I wasn't buying it anymore. I was tired, confused, scared, and headed back to my rat infested new home, where I would try to get some rest. This is when I began to realize that the man I loved the most in the world might not be my protector after all. In fact, he was looking more and more like the enemy. These are not easy thoughts for a young man who was incapable of taking care of himself. The reason I could not take care of myself is because my father wanted it that way. I was his property and I knew it.

Another time, when he wanted to sneak out of the house at night (but thought the police might be watching), my father asked me to act as a diversion. He had me put on his trench coat and carry a briefcase, then walk out to his car, get in and leave. He was hoping that they would mistake me for him and follow me so that he could slip out in my stepmother's car. He said there was no risk for me in this because they would simply see they made a mistake. The idea sounded reasonable, but the last time I tried to help him, I spent the night in jail. I was beginning to realize that I was expendable.

There was one other new fear that I have failed to mention in all of this. As the past was revealed to be a complete illusion, I was also losing *my future*. In the midst of all this it was becoming abundantly clear that I had no future. Not only was everything I knew disappearing, but all of my hope was going with it. This was all happening over a very short period of time, five to six months.

During this time, it became virtually impossible not to see the truth about my dad. His mask was being removed, and I didn't like what I saw. He was empty inside, dark and cold with no compass. The mask is what I had been clinging to since the day that I was born. It wasn't just any illusion: this was the one that allowed me to idolize the enemy himself and seek shelter, comfort and refuge in the very presence of what I should be *running from*.

The final straw, the one that broke the camel's back, for me, and overloaded my ability to process this came the day before my father was scheduled for his sentencing hearing. This is the memory with which I had the most trouble. It wasn't until recently that I was able to recall the final bits and pieces of this memory and begin to understand why it was such an elusive memory for so long. It wasn't the scariest thing that happened to me, but how and when it happened made it a deal breaker for my capacity to accept all this.

My dad attempted to have me shoot him in the ass with a shotgun to avoid his sentencing on the land fraud charges. We got in the car together and he began to tell me his plan. We were going to drive out in the woods together and he told me that I was going to shoot him in the ass with a shotgun. He said we would say it was an accident, and it would keep him from having to go to the sentencing the next day.

He said, "Do you understand what I'm telling you son? If you don't do this they are going to take me away tomorrow!" He said this over and over as I began to crumble. He could see that I was having a problem with this, and it only made him more demanding. He told me again, *"Do you understand what I'm telling you, son? If you don't do this, they are going to take me away tomorrow! Do you understand me son?!"*

I was unable to pull the trigger and became the target of my father's anger and frustration. At that time I still wanted to believe that my father was the man that I knew, and I was crushed by not being able to meet his expectations.

Apparently, I called a friend that night. My friend said I was crying when I called to tell him of this story. He remembered me as being devastated. He and I never spoke of this again, and I did not remember the event at all until he told me about it twenty years later in 2004 after hearing the story of my recovered memories related to the double murders my father committed. This memory was completely hidden from me for years. It has taken work to find it, and now I understand why.

I remember the feeling of holding a shotgun pointed at my father, of being asked to shoot him. He was leaning on a fence post encouraging me to pull the trigger. I was already overwhelmed by all that was happening with my father's impending sentencing. Being asked without notice to shoot my father was too much for me to shoulder, and I broke down, crying hysterically. I begged him not to make me do it. The sight of me crying and begging made him sick.

He turned around, disgusted, walked toward me and grabbed the shotgun from my hands. He then, very briefly, yet forcefully, pointed the shotgun at my face and said, "Maybe if I just shoot you, that will work." At that very moment I thought that he was going to kill me. He wanted to shoot me, I could tell, but he caught himself.

The ride home was the worst. He tried to show me some pity and told me that he was just kidding about shooting me. He asked if I understood that and I meekly said "Yes Dad, I'm sorry I couldn't do it." I was now a complete failure. He was possibly headed to prison the next day, and this was our final time together. It would be my fault if they took him away the next day. All of my weaknesses were completely exposed to my father, and he was disgusted. Here I was, stripped down in front of my father to a shadow of myself, scared, trembling, unable to do what he asked . . . pitiful. I was so worthless, in fact, my own father wanted to kill me.

The next morning he left the house to go to Atlanta for his sentencing. I don't recall much about the night before, only that my friend said I called him. I received the news from my stepmother that Dad had been given twelve years for land fraud and taken straight to county jail. He wasn't coming home, and that was the last time that I spent with him before he left.

At least now I understand why this event was deleted from my memory so quickly. It had so much attached to it, including the clincher of being told that I would be responsible for him going to jail if I couldn't do this. It was simply too much for me to handle at that time.

Over a fifteen-year period my dad made millions by successfully orchestrating elaborate land deals, masquerading as various government agents and assuming the identities of dead people, using the names he found on fresh graves in cemeteries. In this latest case, he forged land titles and other documents in three real estate cons that could have netted him $1.6 million, but finally, he got caught.

He called me collect that night from jail before my stepmother returned, and there was panic in his voice. He kept asking me how much time they gave him, and I told him it was twelve years. He kept saying, "What?" as if he could not hear me. He would later say that it was days before he understood what that meant. For me, it would be years.

I tried to *be a man* while we were on the phone and did my best to keep it together, but I was a wreck. I began crying uncontrollably the moment we hung up. The only world that I had ever known was gone. It seemed to disappear in the blink of an eye. Dad wasn't coming home.

The events of those two days were too overwhelming for me. I felt like my emotions were about to explode at any minute. They probably would have if I knew what I was feeling. I didn't know which event I was responding to. Was it how I let my dad down the day before? Was it him not coming home? Was it the disturbing call from him, trying to understand what had happened and how many years he was given?

Or was it the fact that I was finally beginning to understand that my father was not who I thought he was?

Chapter 4

Exposed—A Look Behind the Curtain

A short time after my father's sentencing; I decided to move to Miami where my mom lived. I wasn't welcome in my step-mother's house, and I got out of there as quickly as I could. I was still reeling from all the events leading up to my dad's sentencing. Everything seemed to be happening so fast, and it wasn't slowing down just because he was gone. Things were spinning out of control.

Now I had the added fear of not having a future or even a place to live. I hadn't given it that much thought. I was a little pre-occupied with the rapid collapse of the only world that I had ever known. I was not prepared for any of this.

I moved in with a close friend of mine from high school. His parents were a ray of light in all this madness. They provided some stability and hope. My mom lived in a one-bedroom apartment, but neither of us was ready to live together. That would come later, but for now I was simply trying to find my way and so I moved in with my friend.

During this next phase of my life, I would learn that Mom had lung cancer and would watch her die. I would try to execute an extraordinary and legitimate land deal for my father that could have made millions. I would also experience my first serious attempt at suicide.

This bad dream was my new reality. Actually, it was becoming apparent that I had always lived in a nightmare. It was time to take a closer look at the dark figure who ruled over the bad dream.

I remembered some articles *The Miami News* had written about my dad when I was thirteen, so I thought the Miami Public Library would be a good place to start my search. When I entered the building, the first thing I noticed, centered in the middle of the library, was a painting of my grandfather, E Clyde Vining. It was in recognition of him being the youngest President of the Florida Bar Association in the state's history. It was surreal.

The Miami News articles were always in the back of my mind. I couldn't remember what all the attention was about, but I did remember vividly my father's response to them. I was just a young boy, but that didn't keep him from talking to me about it. He had all the newspapers neatly arranged on the floor of his office so that every headline was showing. There must have been ten to fifteen articles. The headlines were about windfall profits from secret land trusts where a speculator made hundreds of thousands of dollars by defrauding land owners and the state government. The trail was hidden behind these secret land trusts, but everything pointed to one guy—Dad.

He showed them to me when I was in his office and said, "I'm going to sue those bastards." He said they were out to get him because he was a successful guy and they didn't like that. How dare they bring all this attention on him! They were going to pay, all of them. He said that he kept the articles in full view as a constant reminder of what they tried to do to *him*.

He especially hated the *The Miami News*. "Run by a bunch of no good, dirty rotten Jews," he used to say. Even at that age, I had a problem connecting the dots. When his rationale made no sense to me, I just put it out of my mind. I must have been practicing this from a very early age because I was good at it.

Now it was time to go back and figure out what all the fuss was about. Suddenly Dad didn't look like the innocent victim anymore, and I wanted to learn more. In fact, as I began to think more about it, there were signs everywhere. *The Miami News* stories just happened to be the easiest place to start.

The library kept old newspapers on microfilm back then. Because I had to guess at the year, I went through a lot of old microfilm before I found what I was looking for. As scary as this was, it was equally exciting. When I finally found the first story, I lost my breath and almost froze in anticipation of what I might learn. This suddenly became real and very personal. For the first time I was beginning to understand who my father really was.

What I didn't realize at the time was what else this was doing to me. Opening the door to *who* my father was led me to a bigger, even scarier question. *What* exactly, *is* my father?

For now, I focused on the stories and what he did. It was fascinating. Basically, he made hundreds of thousands of dollars by buying large tracts of land, then optioning them to the state for construction rock pit sites. The Department of Transportation mined gravel from these sites to build an extension for the South Florida Turnpike.

The problem was that before he bought them, dad knew in advance that the state was looking for these sites to dig out landfill to build the toll road. The unsuspecting landowners had no idea that the state was in line to offer them huge sums of money. My father came between the two parties and cleverly used the state's option fees to buy the land for himself. Knowing the state wanted it, Dad purchased an option to buy the land, then sold the mineral rights of the site to the state and used the money from the state to purchase it.

The options brought in almost five times more than what he paid for the land and after the state dug out the landfill the property actually increased in value. The huge hole left behind filled up with water and the land became lakefront property. That is how he marketed it. The plan sounded very smart to me, except for one little detail. It was illegal and unethical.

My father was the mastermind behind this scheme, but he was not alone. He involved politicians, bankers, friends and associates to cover his tracks. He also used his real estate license to make commissions on the sale of the property, using secret land trusts to protect the identity of the owner—him.

It was fascinating to me how he orchestrated this whole thing. In a weird sort of way, I think I was proud of how he pulled this deal off. I knew it was wrong, but something about this whole experience was very revealing to me. I was beginning to see my father as two different people. Not consciously, of course, but I was unable to put the two together in the same thought and this caused my emotions to fluctuate all over the place.

Janet Reno was the Assistant State Attorney at the time, and she spearheaded the probe. I remember my father talking about her. His description of her was not pleasant, and he attributed many of the qualities that he emphasized to the fact that she was a woman. I knew that my father didn't think much of women, but this was heavy, serious stuff that he was trying to teach me. Again, I just wasn't making the connection, and I dismissed it. I figured I simply didn't get it, and I tried not to think about it.

As I researched these stories, some frightening issues kept coming up. Was anything that my father told me the truth? If he said these awful things about this woman, but he was the bad guy, what did that mean to me? For me, the fascination was beginning to wear off. It was raising more questions than it seemed to be answering. I no longer liked the way this was making me feel, so I made copies of the articles and left the library.

As it turned out, my father's only punishment was that he had to give up his real estate license. I remember him telling me about that. He gave testimony under protest in the case, then sued to prevent its use and won. He gave up his license under pressure, he said, just to show them he didn't care, because it restricted his ability to operate like he wanted to anyway. Boy, would that turn out to be a self-fulfilling prophecy!

I lived with my friend for a few weeks as things began to settle. My father stayed in constant contact with me, writing or calling me collect from prison, and I would occasionally visit him. They first sent dad to a minimum security prison in the Florida Panhandle, and I visited him a few times there.

All this time he was re-establishing our relationship. I didn't know it at the time, but that is what was happening, and I was all too willing to go along. He was building me back up again, telling me what I wanted to hear. He never apologized for what had happened, but often said how he became desperate, and messed up. Not to worry, he explained. He was going to straighten it all out. Part of the straightening would require my involvement, and I was excited to have another chance to prove to my dad that I was worthy of his love.

Just before my father left for prison, he had begun to tell me about a land deal that he was working on. It involved thousands of acres right across the center of the state of Florida. Even though I was skeptical, it made perfect sense to me. In fact, it sounded like the deal that he had prepared his whole life for.

In the 1960s the state condemned thousands of acres across the state to build a barge canal. The idea was to create a waterway where barges could cross the state and save the days of travel that it takes to go all the way around the bottom of Florida.

After years of failed attempts to build the canal, the project was finally halted because of the unanticipated damage that it would do to Florida's underground aquifer. Studies found that the drinking water in our state would become contaminated, and construction stopped.

The landowners were suing the state to get their land back since it was condemned for this purpose, and they were winning. They only had to pay the state back the same money that the state had paid them when it was taken in the 1960s. My father was studying this situation and learned that there were also thousands of acres condemned in the 1930s.

As he researched, he found that the state paid only two dollars per acre at the time for the land. He estimated that some of the land was now worth as much as two thousand dollars an acre. The state paid four thousand dollars for the acreage and now, in 1984, it was worth four million. He wanted it.

His plan was to find the rightful heirs to the property and seek to represent them in a lawsuit to get the land back. He would offer the heirs twenty-five to forty percent depending on the situation. The idea was that it was found money to them and they would have no idea how to do it on their own . . . and he was right.

This plan made sense to me and seemed straight up. My father built me up as the savior to the whole family and armed me with records, maps and contacts. The one thing he didn't have was money. I would have to find someone who could help to pay for me to spend a few months on this project, but I was the guy. I was relieved to have a second chance with my father and thought this would change everything if I could pull it off. This was my chance to save the family and get rich at the same time. I had something new to focus on and I buried the past. I set out to fix everything that was wrong in my life, including my father.

I presented this idea to my friend's parents, hoping that they might be interested. It was very difficult, and I understood what I was up against. This was a tough sale, but I had all the records to prove the plan would work, including all the original landowners and information on the current court cases. Finally, an old girlfriend's parents agreed to help. I am not sure if it was pity, a loan or a long shot investment for them, but it bought me three months in Ocala, Florida where I could spend my time becoming familiar with the land, searching probate records and looking for the original landowner's heirs.

The drive to Ocala was a long lonely ride, but I was full of hope again. I so wanted to believe that this would work. My stepmother was even talking to me again, hoping that this might save the family. My dad was broke when he got sent away, and my stepmother was already losing the expensive house that they lived in.

I lived in Ocala for a couple of months and made some progress. I was locating the heirs to the property and even set up a meeting with a huge law firm that was representing multiple cases from the 1960s condemnations. We were hoping to piggyback on his cases and move right through the courts. It looked as if everything was really coming together, and I was excited. My father would call me every few days for an update and tell me what a good job I was doing. He was directing me from prison, and it felt so good to hear those words from my father again. I loved our talks about how great things were going to be and how proud he was of me.

Everything was falling into place, and some of the original landowners agreed to sign on, then we suddenly hit a snag. The state created a new district court that took jurisdiction on the new cases, and they were sent to a different court of appeals. All of the rulings that gave the land back had been upheld, but now everything rested on this new court's decision.

The new judges didn't agree with the lower courts and reversed the decision. They decided that under the law the state could keep the land even though it was not used for the purpose for which it was originally condemned. Because the two courts had conflicting opinions, the matter would be sent to the state Supreme Court, and a final decision could take years. My heart sank. This was devastating.

Once again the world began to close in on me. Everything had seemed within reach, but now it was just a pipe dream again. I suddenly was out of a job, but that wasn't all I was out of. I was out of hope and money too. I was going to have to go back to Miami with my tail between my legs and with no prospects.

The Saturday afternoon before I was to pack up, I watched a football game by myself. It was my favorite team, the Florida Gators. They had a chance to win their conference for the first time in school history. The game was a welcome distraction, but the Gators played awful from the start. It was painful to watch and just made me sicker. I had a lot to drink and finally decided I just didn't want to feel this pain anymore.

I had fantasized about suicide many times before, but never really seriously considered it. The thought would come and go, depending on how things were with my family. I was lost and never really felt like I fit in. My life had always been a charade, but now I had nothing to hide behind. I was exposed for what I really was. I felt like a weak, sniveling, scared little boy. It made me sick, and I wanted it to all stop.

I planned it out pretty well, I thought. I was definitely serious about it. I placed a small white Styrofoam cooler next to me on the pull-out couch in my small studio apartment. I continued to get drunk and sat with a straight razor next to me, preparing to cut my wrist. I knew this was going to be the hardest part, and I tried to prepare for it. I knew to cut in line with the vein, not across. I am not sure where I learned this, but I must have been interested when I heard it because I had that information stored when I needed it.

I studied my wrist and braced myself. I knew that once this vein was cut, there would be no turning back. I didn't think about what was on the other side; I only wanted relief from this hell. My first try didn't go deep enough. Probably because this was so hard to do to myself that I wasn't pushing hard enough. I tried again, and this time I pushed deep into the vein, the blood began to flow.

I placed my hand in the cooler and lay back on the couch, ready to die. I think I dozed off for awhile from pure exhaustion. Again, I don't remember worrying or thinking about actually dying, just a numbing sense of nothingness. I remember waking up around three A.M. and feeling incredibly hungry. I looked in the cooler and there was about an inch of blood, but that was it. For whatever reason, it had stopped.

I staggered up and went to the store to get some food. There was nothing left in my apartment because I didn't think I'd need it. I remember staring at my wrist as I wrote a bad check for bread and sandwich meat. It was wrapped with white gauze and I felt like everyone could see right through me. I felt totally exposed, like an alien with no place to hide, just hopeless and forced to continue on with this hell.

The next day I had to call my mom and tell her I was headed home in utter defeat. I could hardly get enough energy to push the words out and tried to sound as though I was okay. I was afraid that she would see right through me as well and I tried to make up some story about how I cut my wrist while reaching across a sharp metal object to get something. I told her not to think anything of it, it was just an accident.

My mom must have known. Mothers sense these things, I am sure, but our family was all about hiding secrets. She had her own experiences with suicide, and she probably knew what I was feeling. Suicidal tendencies seemed to be an epidemic around my father.

What we didn't know at the time was that I was headed home to watch her die. I was really looking for relief, but this wasn't getting any easier. I had already lost my father. Mom was next.

When I returned to Miami, I temporarily moved in with my mother. She lived in a one-bedroom apartment and I slept on a pull-out couch. I was twenty-four now. It was tough, but at least I was with my mom. She was an alcoholic, but she had not had a drink for a year or two. It was hard to remember, because she would frequently go for a year or two and then just come home drunk.

My mother was a beautiful woman and did the absolute best that she could, but she struggled mightily. It's no wonder. She knew more than anyone what my father was really like, and it must have been tearing her up inside to watch us kids love and defend him. My own struggles kept me from being a very good son to her, but like her, I did the best that I could with what I had. I love her, I know that.

I would bounce around Miami for a while, changing jobs and places to live. I got in trouble with the law one day and spent two nights in the Dade County jail. I was with some friends, and we stayed up all night doing cocaine. I was drinking a lot and occasionally doing other drugs. I was pulled over at sunrise. The officer found I had a suspended license, then he searched the car. There was drug paraphernalia, but no drugs. But that was enough to charge us all.

Because I didn't believe that they would keep me overnight, I didn't call anyone for help. I was wrong. That sick feeling was becoming very familiar to me. I just couldn't seem to get out of this nightmare, and now my behavior was bringing even more hell upon me.

My mom and uncle finally got me out, and I decided to move back in with my mom. The day she brought me home, I slept on the couch all day and barely spoke a word to my mother. God only knows how she felt, because I wasn't capable of understanding what anyone else was feeling. I was a full time job.

Things seemed to get better for a while, and we began to bond. We would cook out, watch sitcoms, sports and movies together. Our time together was fun and we did laugh a lot, but the dysfunction was never far behind. Looking back, I am extremely grateful for those days with her. She showed a lot of courage. I would not have made it without her. She may not have been there when I was little, but she was there for me during one of the darkest periods in my life. I needed that because there was much more to come and I was about to go it alone.

Mom started feeling really sick, and she didn't seem to be getting any better. She underwent various tests at the doctor's office, and there was some real concern. She was also a two-pack-a-day smoker, and she was coughing more than usual. This was serious, but I never expected what I was about to hear.

I think the doctor must have requested that I come with her, because it was unusual for me to take her to an appointment. I don't remember going there, but I do remember what happened.

The doctor sat us down and was very serious. He asked

some questions, and then he said, "I have some very serious news to tell you." He looked at my mom and told her that she had lung cancer. As that hung in the air for a while, I was sitting next to her. Neither one of us knew what to say. The doctor talked about how far along it was, and the news seemed to be getting worse. The more he talked, the worse it got.

He said she was beyond most treatment options, all of them really. He said there were some things we could do to slow it, but that was it. We sat for a minute, but then I couldn't stand it any longer: I had to know. I coldly asked, "What does that mean? How long does she have to live?" I think he was surprised by how direct I was and simply said, "Six months, at best." He then proceeded to tell us what those six months were going to be like, and I went numb again.

I was so sick that I could hardly think about my poor mother. I was a jerk when you really get down to it, but today I can understand why. I couldn't give my mom something that I did not have, and I was just out of gas. I was not prepared for the events that I had been faced with the past couple of years.

My older sister moved in with us, and we took care of our mother as best we could. We put her in hospice for a few weeks near the end, and then we brought her home for her last few days. She wanted to die at home. We gave her ice cream, tried to watch movies and made her as comfortable as we could, but she was out of it. The cancer had spread to her brain and she was often confused and disoriented.

Watching her die was certainly the hardest thing that I had ever done, which is saying a lot. I couldn't bail out on this one. I had to man up as best I could and be there for her. I no longer regret the past, but I do wish I had been better prepared to help my mom in this situation. We'll just leave it at that.

My sister and I could hear her gasping for breath in her bedroom as she was slowly dying. My sister was by her side the whole time. I would leave for a few hours at a time to get a break, but we were both there at the end.

My mother was in so much pain, I was certain that when

she died I would feel relieved. One day that heavy breathing sound just stopped, and that was it. She passed at home in her bed, which is what she wanted. She died a few days after Christmas.

But I was not relieved at all. That is not what I felt, not even close. What I felt was an overwhelming sense of loss. I cried hysterically at the funeral. It was a beautiful service, one that my sister and I planned carefully to make it special for Mom. Still, when it was over, that empty feeling returned to the pit of my stomach and settled back in.

I remember standing on the balcony of my mom's apartment after the service. It was in the afternoon and the weather was beautiful. There were some friends and family inside, and you could hear the faint chatter of their voices. As I sat on the balcony, a strange sense of calm settled over me. It was like nothing I had ever known before. For that brief period, everything seemed okay . . . no, everything was perfectly okay. I felt it and knew it to be true. It was peace. As my mind quieted and rested, I felt complete relief from the constant pressure that I had been under. Something about that moment gave me incredible hope for the future.

That was important, because I was going to need it. I was headed to Orlando to prepare for my father's release from prison. Something had happened along the way that caused my father to be sent to the Atlanta Penitentiary. He was now doing hard time, and it was changing him.

I was about to come back for more; and without the memories, who could blame me? Imbedded in this terrifying experience was one of the most wonderful spiritual secrets and life-lessons ever revealed to me. *I was now the one who needed fixing, not him.* As long as I denied myself help, I would keep going back for more. It came very close to costing me my life.

Chapter 5

Seventeen Months with a Serial Killer

The Killing Year

Repressed memories are a controversial subject for some, but not for me. This behavior is a human survival mechanism. In this case, the act of disassociating specific memories from my awareness may have produced the opposite effect. Repressing memories of certain events prior to my father going to jail and of what I learned about him during the time he spent in federal prison allowed me to rehabilitate his image in my mind so I could join him for another seventeen months of hell while he was killing people.

My father was paroled from the Atlanta Penitentiary in April of 1987 after serving three and a half years, but there was a mix-up that kept him in custody in a county jail well beyond his release date. It took me a few weeks to get him released.

He was furious and called me every day. I had moved to Orlando a year earlier, after my mom died, to help him get settled. It became my full time job to get him out. I was dealing with bureaucrats, and they didn't care about my father. He was just another convict to them. The harder I pushed on the phone to get through the red tape, the less they helped.

I immediately began to notice that my dad was different. His anger was different, much more threatening. It's difficult to describe, other than to say that his threats did not "feel" like idle threats anymore. Something within me knew that he was being honest when he said certain things about "those dirty rats." He really liked that term. He also called them "lowlife dirty rotten bastards, worthless pieces of shit!"

After finally being released, he spent the night in Georgia before he flew "home" to Orlando the next evening. The night that I met my father at the airport was nothing like what I had imagined it would be. I was hoping that he would be happy to see me and that we would celebrate his coming home. Most of all, I just wanted to hug my dad again.

Some of that night is still a little vague. My half-brother and half-sister were with me, but I don't recall seeing much of them after our little reunion. We were not very close and this whole scene was weird. None of us knew how to react to Dad coming home. We had never really talked about how each of us felt about Dad being in prison in the first place. We certainly never discussed how we felt about him coming home, so this was all very awkward. Some of it is hard to remember because after he arrived, my memory is almost exclusively of my father and me that night. He treated *them* like kids, but he made it very clear from the very beginning that I was with *him*, as if I were already part of his plans. It used to make me feel special when my dad treated me that way, but this was different. I didn't know at the time what that really meant, but somewhere deep down inside of me, I could feel it. It was pulling at me like the undertow of a large wave, one that was about to drown me.

We went out to the gate to meet his plane, but somehow missed him. I have no idea how that happened or why we went to the wrong gate, and he didn't allow us time to figure it out. Once we met up with him, it was all about his plans and he was in a hurry. He was a man on a mission. He was ready to make up for lost time, and fast. Little did I know how much *work* he had done before getting home. He had already set the wheels in motion to murder five people and would be adding more targets to this list along the way. For three of them, their fate was sealed before he left Atlanta.

When we found him in the airport, he was not happy to see us as I had hoped he would be. He was pissed. "What the fuck happened to the big welcome home at the gate?" were his first words to me. He said, "I was expecting a banner and all you kids to meet me when I got off the goddamn plane." We explained that we missed something and went to the wrong gate. He commented about how we "could fuck up anything," that we "had three and a half years to get there on time, but still fucked it up!" Then he relaxed and laughed as he reminded us that he was home now. He was going to fix everything, including us. He made it abundantly clear.

He started talking immediately about his plans. He was headed to Miami and Naples to get some money from two of his brothers, visit his mother, pick up her car and begin his "plans". Right now he just needed money. He expected everyone to jump now that he was out. He always felt that other people's money belonged to him and that is one characteristic that had not changed in prison. In fact, he thought we all owed him.

I vividly remember being in my car with him after leaving the airport. He looked at me and told me that I was fat and needed to lose weight, but he was going to fix that. He also didn't like it that I was a tending bar at twenty-six years old and that my car was a "piece of shit," but he was going to fix that as well. He was home, and everything was back under his control now. This feeling too, was indescribable. His words made it sound like he only wanted the best for me, but the controlling nature of his comments and his tone were unnerving as hell. On the surface everything seems that *it should* be great, but underneath something is very wrong. You kind of feel it, but dismiss it because you can't rationalize the feelings. I had become very good at dismissing feelings that I could not rationalize. My father was giving me plenty of new opportunities to perfect this odd behavior that I had developed as a child.

He was home, but it didn't feel right. I had dreamed and wished for this moment, but now that it was finally here, there was something in me that instinctively knew that this was all bad. This dream was a nightmare. Maybe it was just an adjustment period, I thought. Maybe prison had temporarily hardened him and he'd change back soon, I tried to convince myself. I was looking for my dad, not realizing that this guy and my dad were one and the same. He hid much of his real character from me when I was a kid, but he wasn't interested in hiding his true self from me anymore. No, he was interested in getting busy, and I knew from his comments that he owned me. The homecoming didn't go well, and that was just the beginning. I was the one that was in for an adjustment period.

One of the first memories that I have of my father showing a complete disregard for risk was shortly after he returned home. He was quickly running out of the money his brothers had given him, and he was becoming desperate.

Apparently, he received an insurance check for the guy that used to live in the apartment that he rented. It was from a large insurance company and was for a small amount of money. He took the check to a copy store. He copied the check and it looked the same to him. He said he was in total disbelief that this could be so easy. These color copiers were new to him.

He then changed the amount to around ten thousand dollars and the payee on the copied check to John Vining. He copied it again, this time with the new amount and his name. He practiced this for a while so he could get it just right. He really liked these new copiers. It was as if someone had given him an unfair advantage while he was away. He laughed at how easy it was. Forgery was not new for Dad. In fact, he was a master at producing forgeries. That was his specialty and that's what he did time for. He forged deeds and stole other people's land for a living.

He said that it was a big insurance company and that it would take them forever to notice something was wrong and to figure it out, if they ever did. The bank cashed the check, he said, "Because I'm a harmless old fart with a retired Air Force ID, and nobody would believe that I would do something so crazy." He was so proud that he had talked them out of holding it for five to seven days. He said he went right to an officer of the bank and made up some story about what the check was for and why he needed it cashed the same day. The face-to-face interaction was the fun part for him. He left that bank with more than ten thousand dollars in cash for a copy of a check he had doctored with a copy machine.

I could see him light up as he described this. He even showed me copies of the check and said he might wallpaper his apartment with it. He laughed so hard at times that his eyes were watering. This was fun and exciting to him. He believed that he was smarter than *them* and that they had a problem. You see, he didn't operate with boundaries anymore. One of his favorite new sayings was how they were now paying for sending him to "Pen State", referring to his time in the state penitentiary.

The first problem that I had with this was how freely he told me about it. I mean he was proud of it. I acted calm when he told me, but the truth was that this stunt was incredibly disturbing to me. It appeared that he couldn't see any connection with what he did and "their" ability to catch him. He used his own name on the check without fear of the consequences. It simply wasn't a concern anymore. He said it was just a matter of time before he scored big and then he would be untouchable.

He didn't seem to have any boundaries and that worried me. The rules had changed since he came home. He used to try to keep things in check and risk at a minimum. Not anymore. That, in fact, was his new edge he said. No rules would make it impossible for them to figure him out. What I didn't really understand yet is that he was preparing for his first murder, that of an old friend and long-time associate.

These small crimes, and there were many of them, were only reinforcing his belief system and giving him confidence. Now, looking back, I can see it. Each *victory* fueled him as he moved deeper and deeper into executing his new plan. His new plan and strategy on the big deals was simple. Don't leave witnesses.

This is where I began to add another new behavior. I had to learn not to act surprised when he gave me glimpses of his world. I was learning on the fly because things were unraveling fast and he was studying me carefully. I could tell. I tried to keep cool on the outside, but inside I was all panicked.

What the hell was he doing and what would he do if I told him I thought something was wrong with his behavior? Words simply cannot describe this feeling. There is no manual that teaches us how to handle these experiences in life. I began to move into survival mode. I knew I was being given a pass into a world I shouldn't see, but I was afraid to say I wasn't interested. The thought of what he would do if I disapproved was one I could not entertain. Every time I came close to that thought, I quickly dismissed it.

You see, there was a bigger problem for me. Dad had begun to tell me about a land deal he was working on with his old friend and associate. He was carefully and slowly telling me more and more. He was testing me, no doubt.

He had set up another fake land deal. He explained it to me, but I didn't understand how it would work. There was a piece of property in the Keys that his friend owned, and somehow my dad said he would soon own it outright. He was carefully and purposely leading me to ask him The Question.

In another one of those "trying-to-rationalize my feelings" moments that I now remember clearly, I accepted his invitation. Even though I didn't want to know the answer, I still asked the question. I was afraid not to accept his invitation to know more, so I asked, "Why would he let that deal happen?"

We were in his car riding through Apopka, a small farming community northwest of Orlando. This memory, for some reason, is in slow motion. As he drove down Rock Springs Road, I could see the trees and pastures going by beside him, outside the driver side window. I was in the passenger seat, feeling very uncomfortable in this conversation and trying not to show it. I was desperately trying not to show it. In fact, I was wishing that I was not there and hoping that it wasn't real. I already knew where this conversation was headed. I kept dismissing the thought in my mind over and over, but the conversation with my father kept heading toward something I really didn't want to hear. It was that runaway train again. That undertow. I wanted a "take back" so bad that I couldn't stand it. He was going to tell me something that would change everything, forever. *Don't do this Dad, please don't do this* is all that I was thinking. *Please, someone, please don't let him say this.*

The trees passed by in the car window behind him in slow motion, almost as if we were completely separated from the outside world. The inside of the car suddenly took on the feeling of a prison, where I became the prisoner and my father the guard. It seemed like it had always been that way; I just hadn't noticed it before. He began to speak, carefully, but with absolute confidence in what he was sharing. He simply explained that there would be no witnesses. He said, "He won't be around to dispute the deal." These words hung in the air as they slowly solidified our relationship and bonded us together in time. I was now his, and he was now mine. No more chances to lie to myself about my dad. He did for me what I could not do for myself . . . he pulled back the curtain and showed me the truth.

The plan was set and the deal almost done. It was clear to me that he was very proud of his ability to tell me he was going to do this, almost as if it had elevated him to another level, above the rest of us. I think that is why he told me. It was because he couldn't help himself. That's how good he thought his new plan was. He didn't say outright that he was about to kill his friend, but it was crystal clear to both of us what he was saying. These dark revelations were becoming more and more difficult to dismiss. This one was a problem, a big problem.

I'd like to say that I considered running from him or calling the police, but I don't remember anything that I thought or did after I left him that day. Maybe I dismissed it quickly, I

don't know. I may recall it one day, but these things take time.
I know that now. Even now, the picture is still coming together
as I write this and not everything is clear yet. Part of the
problem is where the lines begin to blur together, between
what I did, what I knew and what he made me do. These are
things that we have to settle for ourselves and it takes work.

My father was working me into this plan from the very
beginning; it was always in his mind that I would help him.
When he was in the penitentiary, he had already planned to kill
five people, and I was his *go for*. It was no accident that I was in
Orlando to help him. He didn't care what it took to show them
that they had wronged him, even if he had to use his own son
to set it all up. And that's exactly what he did. He believed that
he was untouchable, and it was time for them to pay. It was
Showtime.

Bob Ragen disappeared on May 31, 1987. He had gone to
Orlando to meet with my father with the signed deed to sell
property in the Keys for cash to some Columbians. There were
no Columbians, just a harmless old fart. This is a deal that my
father was supposedly arranging to help his *friend* out while he
was in the penitentiary.

My dad now had the deed, but he did not have the money
needed to record it, which I remember was around thirteen
thousand dollars. At one point he *convinced* me to ask some of
my real estate friends to buy into the deal in order to get the
deed recorded.

The lines were beginning to get very blurry for me. Now I
was seeking the help of guys I knew to invest in property that
was related to a murder. I met with some friends and tried to
explain some rational reason why my dad had it and couldn't
afford the doc stamps, but my heart wasn't in it and nothing
came of it. I am pretty sure that I sabotaged it that day. I was
not very convincing and I didn't want them involved. I went
through the motions for my dad because I was afraid to come
up with a reason not to. Sounds insane and it is, but that's the
way it was. If he wanted something, he could work me into a

box that made it seem there was no other alternative, no matter
how insane of a proposition it was.

This plan made me sick to my stomach, and I was more
confused than ever. Was I participating in this? My father was
so good at manipulating people and his hold over me was so
complete that I really couldn't tell the difference anymore—
except for the way it made me feel. I felt spiritually bankrupt
and dead inside. I was giving up all hope in such a thing as
Goodness. It was just too hard to fight that dark powerful
undertow that was now sucking the life out of me.

This total surrender might have actually helped me some,
because this particular nightmare was just beginning. I started
working very hard to try and "accept" this situation as it was
because there wasn't enough information to stop him. I began
trying to rationalize, hoping to work it out as quickly as I could
so that I could continue to live with myself. The problem was
that my father's murderous behavior was moving much faster
than my ability to lower my values and expectations of this
world.

As for the money needed to record the deed? Dad finally
came up with a solution to get some cash. He was so proud of
how he executed his brilliant plan that he couldn't resist
sharing this one with me, too.

A few months after the land deal, we were drinking a
couple of beers at a table in Applebee's restaurant. He had
some good news and was excited to see me. He was overflowing with excitement and pride. He had some money for
me, too.

My father liked to surprise people with good news, and he
smiled as he handed me what I remember to be about five
thousand dollars. I really needed money and thought this
would help relieve some of the pain that I was feeling. I was
extremely happy to see all this money, and for a brief moment
I felt that everything was okay. Then I asked him how he got it.
Why did I just ask that question? I thought to myself.

Apparently, I hadn't learned my lesson because I suddenly

felt like I did that day in the car with him. It was "déjà vu all over again". Everything slowed down as he asked if I really wanted to know. It sounded like a question, but it really wasn't. My heart and mind said no, but I said yes. He asked if I was sure as though this was something extremely sensitive, and again I said yes.

I didn't want to hear the answer, but I couldn't say it. That thought was frozen and I couldn't get the words out. Part of me wanted to know, but deep down I knew that this was going to be worse than the last time I asked a question like that. I was already feeling sick again, but I couldn't show my dad. I was beginning to panic inside. I steadied myself, focused on my beer and listened. He said he stole the money from "a couple of dirty n----- drug dealers".

He said that he set them up to believe that he had a large amount of cocaine buried out in the woods. He told them the coke came into his possession by some sort of fluke accident, and he had no idea what it was worth. He told them he didn't know anything about drugs and just wanted to get rid of it. The price he gave them was about one quarter of what it was worth. He said they fell all over themselves trying to take advantage of him, and that they thought he was a stupid old white guy who didn't know what he had. *This was the con.* It was they who didn't know what they had, but they couldn't resist it. Of course, there was no cocaine, and my father knew exactly what they would think it was worth. This was easy, he said. He absolutely loved to play the old fart role and use their greed as motivation. He was going to pay them back for "trying" to take advantage of an old fart like him. They were the bad guys, according to him.

He said he picked them up at the airport. They were wearing sports jump suits and a lot of jewelry. He played up the dumb white guy role as they drove out to the woods where he told them the cocaine was buried. They walked to a spot by a pond, and he said to dig there. They were all three together. As the men were digging, my father told them that he needed to go back to the car to get another shovel to speed things up. He casually walked back to the car and opened the trunk as they continued to dig. He said he was very calm.

He wasn't getting a shovel. No, he had a shotgun in the trunk. He said he leaned in the trunk, pulled out his shotgun, took aim and fired killing one of the black guys. He said he dropped him immediately. He then pumped and shot the other guy in the shoulder and neck area, but he said, "I didn't kill the son of a bitch and he ran." The level of excitement in my father's voice increased dramatically as he told the rest of the story. He said, "Shit, I didn't kill that bastard, and I thought he was going to get away." He laughed at his inability to hit his target.

The next part was described with great pride. He brimmed with satisfaction and the delight of his own intelligence at how he improvised.

He figured the other guy had nowhere to go, so he went to the car, started it and backed it out of the woods. He made sure the other guy, if he was watching, thought he fled the scene. He parked the car and began to slip back into the woods towards the spot where he had murdered the first guy. He explained how proud he was because he used his turkey hunting experience to slip back up on the wounded number two guy. As he quietly settled in, his shotgun pointed directly at the spot where they had dug the hole, sure enough the second guy came sneaking back to see his friend. My father patiently waited until he returned to the spot and "dropped him," as he put it. This time he didn't miss. "That dumb son of a bitch came right back to the same spot, just like I knew he would." My father was giddy and excited.

Normally he would be watching my reaction to see if I was accepting of his behavior, but not this time. He was too full of himself to worry about what I thought. "How dare they think that they could take advantage of an old fart like me," he repeated. He had made them pay for that, and he felt good about it. He was lost in the excitement of what he was feeling as he relived it.

I stared at my beer and desperately tried to rationalize what was happening. It wasn't computing and I was stuck. I couldn't wait to get away from him, but instead, I had to act happy for him. He would later say that he "remembered celebrating that moment with me." I wasn't celebrating. I was drifting, drinking and looking for relief from this pain. I was alone in this nightmare and couldn't tell a soul. I didn't know who these guys were, where they were from or exactly where this had happened. No bodies, no names, no crime scene? He withheld just enough information to protect himself.

After we left the restaurant, he took me out to the parking lot to show me the rest of the cash. He opened his trunk and showed me a black bag that contained about twenty-five to thirty thousand dollars. I mustered a smile. I wanted to throw up, cry, call for help, and yell. It was just me and my dad living together in some kind of vacuum.

My dad had been out of prison five months and had already killed three people. This didn't look like a "one off" situation anymore. There was a pattern developing here, but I was terrified to think about it. It was absolutely impossible for me to get my mind around it as I continued to search frantically for answers.

Looking back, I did exactly the opposite of what I should've done. I turned away from God instead of towards him. I was driving home on I-4 with my mind racing. So many questions and so many thoughts. Could I stop him, who do I call, what do I do now? Then I came back to the bigger question that was on my mind. How on God's earth could something like this happen. How could this be? I was not a faithful person, but surely this couldn't possibly happen if there was a God, right? So right there, I decided that there was no God, couldn't possibly be.

I attempted to rationalize that this was a *nature thing*, the result of evolution and us being animals. My father was simply a predator, and those men were his prey. For the moment, that is how I accepted it. I rationalized this over and over. No God, just nature at work and I had a weird vantage point that most people don't have. He was a predator, that's it. This explanation wasn't going to be good enough to stand the test of time, but at least it helped me survive that night.

I was so exhausted from all of this that I just couldn't muster the strength to block it all out any more. I needed to find a way to accept it, and that's the best that I could come up with. I thought I was past the breaking point that night. I didn't believe that I could handle anymore of these surprises, but there were still more to come.

As I tried to deal with all the emotion tied to what I saw and what I did, I came to understand that I too was part of his plan. This is how cold and calculating a sociopath can be. My own father had me set him up in Orlando to start his new profession as a serial killer, and now he was beginning to get me involved, slowly but surely. He was the master, and he manipulated me beautifully to get what he wanted. He planned to have me participate just enough and take just enough money so that I would be scared to go to police. That was his in-surance policy.

In between murders my dad stayed busy. Somewhere in this timeline he came up with another one of his *brilliant schemes* to get some of what he referred to as "walking around money" all the while, he was continuing his attempt to get some money for his new property in the Keys. He had recorded the deed and was now trying to unload the property but he was out of money again.

He found the title to an old Airstream trailer that we once had at a hunting camp. It was maybe ten or fifteen years old and had burned in a fire, but he still had the title. He took the title to the appropriate government agency and explained how the year had been recorded wrong on the title and of course, the agency was more than willing to help such a nice old guy like him out by changing the year for him. He then found a trailer somewhere in Tampa and made it match the numbers and took the title to the bank for a loan. He gave them the location to check it out and he said, "They happily gave me a loan. They would do anything to help an old fart like me out, especially since I am retired Air Force." He pocketed several thousand dollars, and he was having fun. It wasn't a lot of money to him, but he so enjoyed the con. He loved that he could do this. I was observing my father, a guy that had so far killed three people, and he seemed to be having so much fun.

This was definitely a world to which I didn't belong, but it became my reality. And It was becoming increasingly difficult for me to function in the real world at all. I was distancing myself from my friends and everything around me. How do you sit with friends and talk about typical daily stuff when this is your reality? I so wanted to be a part of their world, but I couldn't. There was a heavy force, an energy field around me that was suffocating me and separating me from everything. I was home sick, but didn't have a home to go back to. I was beginning to see that I never had a home here, I never did belong. Thoughts of suicide were becoming very attractive.

A Call for Help Denied

I came home in the late afternoon on December 12, 1987 and turned on the news on before going to work as a bar manager at a local restaurant. We had a sunken living room, and I was standing in the middle of the room when I saw the report. I had been watching the news very closely lately. I got wind of a story about a local woman who had been reported missing and turned up dead, but I wasn't ready for this. There on one of the local news stations, I saw the artist sketch of the suspected murderer. I recognized it immediately: my father.

The enforcement officer had just identified the body of Georgia Caruso, and they described the suspect. They had found her body three days earlier, in the same field where two bodies were found just days before. There had been a local newspaper article about ten days earlier about two skeletons that were found in a field. I read it and was pretty sure that it was the two black guys, but I really didn't want it to be them. If it were them, I might have to do something about this mess and that was a horrifying thought. I tried to put it out of my mind, but here it was in the news. Everything was closing in on me from all directions now.

As I watched the TV, the reporter described the suspect. The description matched my dad. It was also mentioned that he used an inhaler and was driving a Cadillac. That was my dad alright. This murder seemed different. It makes no sense now, but then it did. This was a completely innocent woman. They were all innocent, but this one wasn't involved with my father in any way. Up until then, one of my insane rationalizations was taking comfort in the fact that the guys my father had killed were somehow bad guys because of their backgrounds. That rationalization vaporized the moment that I saw this beautiful woman's picture on the news. I was out of excuses. I felt exposed, vulnerable and defenseless—with nowhere to hide.

The only excuse left was the terror that I felt when I thought about what my dad would do to me if I tried to turn him in, and they didn't lock him up right away. I was certain that they would question him before they would come close to bringing any charges. If that happened, I was sure that it would lead him back to me.

The news anchor went on to explain that a guy named George Williams had answered her ad in the paper to sell some diamonds. For some reason, after meeting with him a couple of times, she agreed to get in the car with him alone so that the diamonds could be appraised somewhere else. She was found three weeks later in the field with two gunshot wounds to the head.

I watched the story and felt faint. I didn't know what to do. I paced as my mind started racing. What the hell had he done now? This woman did not fit the profile. She was so innocent that it just made no sense. In fact, it finally put me over the edge.

I kept asking myself all kinds of questions. Could I have stopped this? What do I do now? Was I to blame? I didn't understand the timeline of events and didn't want to. I didn't understand that she was murdered before the article in the paper about the two skeletons. All I knew was that I was reading the newspaper one day about skeletons being found in a field, and then I was watching this on the news a few days later while I had stood by and done nothing. This situation was totally out of control, and I didn't like these questions, but this was the opening that I could not deny. I had to do something. I was gripped with guilt, shame and terror as that thought hung in my mind for a few moments. What would I say? Would it work? *What would happen to me if it didn't?* That last question stopped me in my tracks.

I was a blackout drinker, and that is where I was headed that night . . . to oblivion. It had worked before, and I was desperately hoping that it would all just go away. I had several beers and called my boss. He wanted to know why I had to miss work. I told him it was serious, very serious, but I couldn't tell them why. They didn't understand, but I didn't care. I never went back to work there again.

Suddenly, it all became clear to me. Unfortunately, it was crystal clear. My father had visited me a few weeks earlier and said that he was back to being "Dr Jekyll" again. He said he had been "Mr. Hyde" the day before and he was feeling good about it. He was headed to Miami to cash something in. He put his foot on the bumper of the car, raised his head back and laughed. He was feeling very good about himself, and he couldn't hide it. He loved that he could be "Dr Jekyll and Mr. Hyde." That was his edge. Nobody would suspect a nice old fart like him of anything. That's what he said about the little stuff he did, but this is where he really believed it. He was excited. He borrowed one hundred dollars from me and left me the black Cadillac.

The car smelled awful. It had an indescribable and powerful odor. Dad said the dog had a terrible accident and that he had to rip out the carpet and tried to cover up the smell with Brut cologne. I drove that car for almost four weeks.

It's probable that I understood what the smell was when I saw the story, but I couldn't handle it and dismissed that horrible thought as I had so many others. He murdered her in that car and placed her body in the back on the floor. That odor stuck with me, but it would be many years before I could accept and understand what it was.

I also remembered him coming back from his day in South Florida with a smile, laughter and some cash. He paid me back and then some. I don't remember how much money he gave me, but I drank champagne with friends that night. I thought I was celebrating, but the truth is that I was trying to drown the pain and buy companionship. It wasn't working.

After putting all this together, I finally got up the nerve to call him. The drinking wasn't enough to drown out the voices in my head anymore, and I knew it. I had to do something. I paced and paced until I was finally able to pick up the phone. It felt like it weighed a thousand pounds. I thought by telling him what I saw on the news, he would run. I wanted him to run. I was hoping beyond hope that he would somehow suddenly realize how wrong this all was and stop killing people. I asked him to run. I wanted him gone. I thought that would save me from having to do something more about this. At least it would buy me some time.

To my horror, he instead told me to meet him at a hole-in-the-wall bar in Apopka. Not knowing what else to do, I agreed. I had not thought this through, and as I prepared to meet him, I realized just how far in over my head I really was. Through all of this I still felt reasonably safe in the belief that he would not harm his own son, but the stakes were so high that I couldn't deny it any longer. This only worked if I didn't have enough information to harm him, but now that was changing. That realization must have temporarily shut me down, because I have absolutely no memory of the long drive over to meet him that night.

I met him inside the bar. He was wearing blue jeans, a white T-shirt and his brown leather jacket. We talked and had a beer. I remember him taking several very deep breaths through his nose and slowly exhaling through his mouth as if he was trying to calm himself. He also would rub his palms across his eyes and mouth, almost like he was trying to re-adjust his facial expressions. I had seen these mannerisms before. They were a sign of frustration. They were also dangerous and threatening.

He told me to calm down and not to worry. He was very bothered that I was so unnerved about confronting him with this. I could sense the disgust in him over my inability to be calm. It was as if I was letting him down. He asked me specifically what I saw on TV that would make someone believe it was him. I don't think I ever asked him if he did it, it was just understood. He was very calculating in his thinking. He seemed to be settling down. Then he simply told me not to worry and said, "You're overreacting." We finished our beers with some awkward idle conversation, and then we walked outside and switched cars. I left in the rental car and he took the Cadillac.

The drive home only lasted about twenty-five minutes, but it felt like a lifetime. The long and dark winding road gave me plenty of time alone with myself. The questions started again. I kept asking myself what was I doing in this world, and why was this all happening to me. It seemed to me that I was supposed to be able to go to my father for help in life, but he was the bad guy. My father was the boogeyman I had always feared as a little kid. I didn't know anybody in the world that I thought could help me.

When I arrived home, I sat in the kitchen, alone in the dark. I thought and thought and thought. I cried and felt hopelessly trapped. Drinking still wasn't working. This already had a bad ending, what difference did it make? I finally realized that there was only one way out and that I had to do the unthinkable.

I decided to call Central Florida CrimeLine and give them my father's name in connection with Caruso's murder. I knew this was extremely dangerous, but I had to do something to stop him . . . I needed to do something to stop him. I was beginning to feel responsible for all of this madness, and this murder had proved to me that he was totally out of control. I obviously didn't want to believe that, after all, one murder should have been enough to convince me. I wanted the madness to stop on its own because I was too scared to do anything about it. This only added to the guilt and shame that I was feeling.

After the call I cried. I still did not know if I had done the right thing: he was my father. Trying to understand that my father was the bad guy was very difficult to wrap my mind around, and in this case, he wasn't just any bad guy, he was a cold-blooded serial killer. I didn't understand that he was a serial killer at the time, but I knew he wasn't going to stop. In fact, even after this I would continue to have problems with knowing that my father was serial killer. It doesn't make sense, but that was my experience. For now, though, I believed it was only a matter of time before law enforcement would pick him up.

I was wrong.

The next morning my dad called and told me he needed my help. He must have realized that the news story could be a problem, and he wanted to get rid of the car. He was very vague on the phone, and there was a sense of urgency in his voice. He simply told me that I needed to meet him at the entrance to the Florida Turnpike and to follow him. He said he was going to need a ride back.

On the way there the gravity of the situation began to sink in. I was extremely hung-over from the night before. I was wondering if the police had already visited him because of my call. I knew if they had, it would be very obvious to him after our meeting in Apopka why they questioned him. Nothing I had experienced before in my life prepared me for the intensity of the fear I felt that morning.

As I came to the turnpike entrance, I saw his car at the bottom of a small hill at the entrance to the highway. It was black, and because the windows were tinted I could not see inside the car. It may have been just a car, but it was menacing as hell, just sitting there waiting for me, like something straight out of a horror movie.

I followed my dad out to a desolate and isolated place up near Wildwood, Florida. Wildwood is a small rural town in the middle of the state where my grandfather grew up. We drove about sixty miles before he headed off onto an old dirt road that led into the woods. We then came to a deep rock pit in the middle of nowhere. As I followed him down into the pit, my heart started to race again. *Was this a con, too?*

Every move my dad made that morning reminded me of the way he tricked the two black guys and how he pulled the shotgun out of the trunk to kill them. As I nervously watched his every step I came to the realization that if this was it, I wouldn't be able to stop him from killing me. He was simply too good at hiding his motives from his victims. I would never see the end coming, no matter how hard I studied his behavior.

This moment of truth revealed something I already knew, but I had been denying. My very life was in the hands of a cold-blooded murderer. The call the night before had exposed it for what it was. The fact that I was his son would have no value in this situation if he knew that I had betrayed him. I was helpless and hopeless in his presence.

He always carried what he called his "goody bag", which held his inhaler, mouth wash and prescription drugs such as valium. He would ask me if I wanted something when we would get together. He must have known that I needed the valium to handle the situations that he was making me a part of, and he was all too willing to accommodate this new habit of mine. When I pulled up next to him and we exited the cars, he offered me some valium and I gladly accepted. I took two and couldn't wait for them to take effect.

He pulled several plastic bottles of charcoal lighter fluid from the back seat of his car and set them on the hood of the rental car. He asked me to stand back as he filled the Cadillac with the liquid. He emptied most of it on the back seat and floorboard. He then lit the car and continued to spray the fluid on the fire as it spread. I tried to keep him in full view by standing behind him at all times.

The heat was intense, and it was spreading at a rapid rate. The entire car became engulfed in flames. I was relieved to see his attention so focused on this task and not on me, but I suddenly panicked at the thought of the car exploding. I tried to get his attention and warn him, but he was completely hypnotized by the whole experience. He was enjoying the thrill of it all. He looked exhilarated as I backed away. Once again, I was terrified. This was becoming my natural state.

Once he realized the risk, he snapped out of it and said, "Let's get the hell out of here." We jumped in the rental car, and as we left the pit. We could see this huge plume of black smoke rising up into the sky. It was incredible. My dad didn't seem to be bothered by the attention that it might bring; he was more interested in what he was feeling from this whole experience. I found relief in that because it led me to believe that this was all he was after today. Maybe I was safe for now. The valium was beginning to work, and I sat back in the seat, exhausted and relieved. He looked at me as though we were in this together and said, "Wow, that was close. Did you see that?" He began to laugh at himself while he described the intensity of the fire. He was having fun again.

On the way home he tried to express some sympathy for what I had been through the past two days. He said, "Sorry to get you involved like this, son. If something happens, I'll try to protect you." He then went on to ask if the money that he had been giving me was helping me. In this brief conversation he summed up our entire relationship for me: *You're involved in this . . . you need me . . . and you owe me.*

It wasn't until writing and journaling about all this that I began to understand that he wanted me there. He needed me there. He sensed my weakness and fear that night and decided a little help from me with destroying evidence used in a murder might be just the insurance policy that he needed. I know that now because I could feel his hold over me increase that day.

On the way home we stopped and got a cake for my younger brother, who was celebrating a birthday. We went to the apartment, and all I can remember is being totally exhausted from the twenty-four hours of pure hell that started with that news story. I had called the police and then spent the day with my father, burning the car and then pretending to act as if everything was okay for my little brother. Words simply cannot describe what this felt like for me. I didn't know that there were different degrees of hopelessness that led to some kind of bottomless pit, but I was sinking even deeper into the abyss. I felt the emptiness deep in my soul increase a little more that day, and I wondered where it all might stop.

I am not sure why the police never questioned my father after that call, but it is on record. A police cruiser came to my house after I called that night, and the officers asked me if I wanted to tell them anything more. I refused. They seemed to understand and didn't press the issue. I thought they would follow up on it, but I was wrong again. Now, after the burning of the car, I wasn't so sure if I wanted them to. I felt that I was living in no mans land where nothing made sense anymore.

There is a memory frozen in time for me that represents the way I was beginning to look at this strange world into which I had fallen. It was a few days after this experience, just before Christmas. I couldn't tell anyone what was happening to me. I felt completely separated from the rest of the world. It seemed that I could watch, but I couldn't participate anymore. I resented that my friends were simply living life as if it were no big deal. It didn't seem fair.

I was renting a house with a couple of girlfriends. One evening I left the house for a walk because I couldn't handle being around them watching them act as if they didn't have a care in the world. It was hard to see them laugh and enjoy themselves. Being carefree seemed so far out of reach that I couldn't even remember what that must feel like anymore. I just couldn't get back there.

I went walking through the neighborhood where we rented the house. It was a nice neighborhood, but nothing fancy. As I came down a hill, my attention was drawn to a tree in someone's front yard, a tree that was lit up with Christmas lights. At first it looked really pretty, but as I began to stare at it, I noticed that the tree was bare. Upon closer inspection, it looked like it was dead.

As I stared at the tree I began to think about how life looked like this to me. Most people see only the pretty Christmas lights and don't realize that the lights are covering up something ugly underneath. It seems that I was the only one who had to see this side of life. Others were still looking at the lights, but I couldn't appreciate them anymore because of what I knew. As best I could tell, the world had always been dead underneath. I just hadn't looked close enough.

The police never did anything with that call I made that night. In retrospect, that probably saved my life, but I would live in his presence with this added fear and sickness through eight more months of hell, all the while my father committed more and more crimes.

I tried not to think about it every time that I had contact with him, but I couldn't control it. Sometimes just the sound of his voice would send my heart into my throat. I never knew when that particular fear would overwhelm me. It was always there, lurking somewhere just under the surface.

Part of me still wanted to believe that he was my father and the unthinkable was not possible, but I now knew the truth. My father would kill me immediately if he found out that I had betrayed him. I would later see this side of him, and it confirmed my suspicion. He would kill me in a heartbeat and enjoy showing me his power up close and personal. But for now, I was conning him, trying to remain cool so that he would believe I was still okay with what he was doing.

One of the few *social* things that we did together was canoeing down the Wekiva River. He had always liked the outdoors, and we would rent a canoe and head up the river with a cooler full of beer. Before my father went to prison, being outdoors—camping and hunting with him—was my favorite thing to do. Now it was extremely taxing. The combination of the fear of being alone with him and the soul sickness of hanging around with a cold-blooded killer had taken all the fun out of the outdoors, as it had everything else that I ever cherished in my life. I was really struggling to survive these little outings. He, on the other hand, was having fun and was always talking about how much money he was going to make on his next deal.

The Love of Money and Torture Lead to Capture

My father killed Caruso out of desperation. He had been unable to sell the property in the Keys and was complaining that Regan had overpriced it. He said, "Regan was an untrustworthy bastard. He got what was coming because he tried to screw me." But now my father had a plan.

First, there was still a problem with the land title. Of course, my father had the solution. He had set up an escaped inmate as an accomplice to help him with another deal that would come later. He decided that he could use him for this deal to solve the problem with the deed.

As I understand it, the deed did not have Regan's sister's signature on it as promised, and my father tried to get it signed by using this accomplice. His new friend posed as a title investigator and tried to convince her to sign some papers. He was instructed by my dad to kill her after he got the signature.

After failing to get the signature, his accomplice refused to kill her as my dad had instructed him, so she narrowly escaped a fatal brush with my father. Had my father been the one to visit her, she would not have been so lucky. Frustrated, Dad forged her signature himself and recorded the document.

He then used a childhood friend of mine to set up a corporation and deeded the property to the corporation. He found a firm in Fort Lauderdale to represent him because he was unable to sell the land, he placed a mortgage on it for close to two hundred thousand dollars. My father originally asked me to be the president of the corporation, and I refused. My friend wound up doing it for the money. My friend was not involved in this deal in any other way, but he was aware that there were issues with it. I had warned him and told him that I refused to do it, but he felt that without any specific facts to support the suspicions, he was just doing my father a favor.

In January of 1988, my father asked me to go with my friend to the loan closing on the property. After some coaxing, I agreed. At this point it just didn't seem to matter any more. Resistance seemed pointless, and I was more afraid not to do it. I didn't know how to get out, and the promise of twenty thousand dollars for a run to Fort Lauderdale seemed as though it might actually ease some of the pain. It did not.

I drove down and spent the night with my friend. It was another one of those strange experiences. On the one hand, I was seeing an old friend, and we were about to get paid fairly handsomely for something very simple. At least it seemed simple, but we were both struggling with it. There was little fear of legal trouble, but there was another law involved for us—one that would not allow me to enjoy this. The evening wound up with a heavy cloud over it and that took the life out of our little reunion.

The next day we went to the closing and sat in a room with a bunch of lawyers and lenders. My dad asked only that I be present and bring the money back. Therefore I sat quietly and just observed. My friend signed all the documents. As usual, the closing had that surreal feeling to it. This was a meeting to conduct business, but I knew that everyone there

was getting tied up in an absolute mess that included a
murdered landowner and a serial killer. I still hadn't placed that
label on my dad yet, but he was stalking other victims, and I
was aware of it.

Sitting in a room like this was the weirdest. This was
where two worlds seemed to be colliding, and I could no
longer tell if I were a witness or participant. These guys were
sitting in their beautiful offices, in their nice suits, about to give
two hundred thousand dollars to a cold-blooded killer for
property that he didn't own, and I was going to deliver the
money. I sat quietly, never introducing myself as the documents were signed. It didn't feel like a good deal to me.

After the meeting we deposited the cashier's check and
began withdrawing the money in increments of nine thousand,
nine hundred dollars to avoid bringing attention from the
government. Apparently the magic number was ten thousand. I
do not recall how much money we withdrew that day, but I
think it was around fifty thousand dollars. I put it in a
briefcase, stopped for some beer and headed back to Orlando.

On the way home, as usual, everything felt all wrong. I
guess if you have a conscience there is just no escaping it. My
conscience was my companion for the long ride back from
Miami that night. I had just purchased my friend's IROC Z28
with cash. This was a car that I had always dreamed of owning.
I had a new car, a briefcase full of money, and I was drinking a
few cold beers. This only added to the suffering—it did not
relieve the pain. I knew this was blood money, and it made me
sick. Plus, I was headed back to Dad, and now he was
celebrating his ability to *help me* again with more money. It was
like old times: *Dad the hero coming to the rescue again.*

Dad spent the money on cars for himself and us kids. He
also gave us some cash. It made him feel powerful to give us
money, and it kept us dependent upon him. He wasted a lot of
it, as he always did, and it was going fast, but he was also
investing in his future.

On November 25, 1987, my father had helped the accomplice escape from a minimum security prison in Alabama. When he met him in prison, my father convinced the prisoner to escape by saying he knew where millions in drug money was buried and he needed his help to retrieve it. This unsuspecting accomplice didn't know it, but when my father picked him up in Alabama, Dad was one week removed from killing his fourth victim. This guy was going to be added to the list as soon as he helped my dad get to the buried money. My father neglected to tell him about that part of the plan, but, that was not the case for me. My dad made sure that I stayed in the loop.

Although the land deal made him happy, it was not what he was after. He wanted more, a lot more, and he had just the plan to get it. Next up was the multi-million dollar treasure buried in Georgia. This one, he talked about a lot. I think he felt comfortable talking about killing drug dealers, or in this case, their wives. He was always telling me how he knew where some big money was buried. He told me how he helped the accomplice escape from prison to help him with this job— another one of his con victims who didn't know he was on my father's to-do list under "don't leave witnesses".

He'd heard a story from a guy he met in the Atlanta Penitentiary, a convicted Georgia drug kingpin, about hiding $3.5 million before he was arrested. The drug dealer was still in prison, but his wife was not. For this job, my father said he needed help. He somehow convinced this guy in minimum security prison to join him. The guy escaped from a minimum security prison in Montgomery, Alabama. My dad was waiting for him when he sneaked out late one night.

It was, of course, the lure of big money that got him. I don't know all of the details, but Dad told me enough. The most important detail, one that he failed to mention to his accomplice, was that he was part of the con too. My father was not going to be sharing the money with him. He was going to wind up dead in a self-dug grave along with the drug dealer's wife.

Dad set him up near where the drug dealer's wife worked, and they started to stake her out. My father was funding this guy and occasionally drove up to Georgia to meet with him. He really liked for the people he was controlling to be dependent upon him for money. He also despised them for it at the same time.

He bought a van and built a cage in the back. The plan was to kidnap her, place her in the cage and torture her until she told them where the money was. This is the deal that my father fantasized about the most. He was convinced that this was his payday, the one that he had been waiting for. It was the perfect set up. Dirty drug dealer with hidden cash that no one could trace. And the amount . . . that was the key. This one was for $3.5 million dollars in cash. Everything else was just to help him get here. This was the deal that he wanted, but he almost didn't make it.

He was running out of money, and he started to lean on me for cash. I had somehow managed to get a great job in the travel industry during all this insanity, and I was beginning to support myself. But Dad wasn't going away. He was still in and out of my life, although not as often. The money from the land deal provided some relief, and I was able to get some space from him, but not for long.

I don't remember why, but apparently I owed him a couple of thousand dollars. I must have borrowed it to keep going until I got the job. He started to lean on me about it and convinced me to sell my car to pay him back. He said that soon he would have more money than he ever dreamed of, and this was temporary. He also had a solution for my transportation needs until he got all that cash. It was another Cadillac.

Sometime during all this my father decided that he wanted a new Cadillac, but he preferred not to pay for it and simply took one. He went to the Cadillac dealership and took one for a test drive . . . alone. "Of course he trusted me, I'm a charming old fart, what could I possibly do?" is how my father described it. He took it for a test drive, but he stopped at a nearby hardware store to have a key made. He waited a couple of weeks and went back late one night to pick up his new car. It was that simple.

Of course there was a risk in driving a stolen car, but he solved that little problem too. He took the registration from my grandmother's Cadillac (you know, the one we burned) and had it changed at the tag agency. He told them there was some mix up, that his car was ten years newer, white and it had four doors instead of two. They changed it right there. They apologized to him. He said they felt bad that such a nice old fart would have so many things wrong with a car registration, but they took care of it.

As I mentioned, after receiving the money from the Keys property I had found some space from my father and was enjoying my new job in the travel industry. I was beginning to believe that I might actually be able to have a normal life after all. This new career in tourism gave me hope, but now my father was becoming dependent on me. Out of money again, he called me one Friday night and asked for one hundred dollars for gas money to get him to Georgia. It was time to roll again. He said he'd bring me back millions for my trouble. His tentacles reached through to my new life and reminded me that I was still connected. It was not over yet.

My father and the accomplice went to Georgia and kidnapped the woman, locking her into a cage they'd constructed in the back of a van. They drove her around for hours, torturing her and demanding to know where the money was, threatening to kill her. My father had knives, guns, a hack saw and a cattle prod in the van. They called out these items off a checklist as they drove her out to the woods. Eventually they left her, handcuffed and bound with duct tape, while they went into the woods and dug a grave.

There was no buried money and in a twist of irony, my father had fallen for a con himself that was about to cost him his freedom. Kids walking through the woods saw my dad and the other man carry the woman from the van. They ran to a nearby convenience store where a couple of off-duty police officers just happened to be shopping. As the kids described what they saw to the police officers at the store, my father drove by in the van and was immediately chased down by police. Other officers went into the woods and arrested his accomplice as he was preparing to kill the woman. These two planned murders would have been numbers five and six. This is the crime that ended his seventeen months of freedom and finally put him back in jail.

On Sunday August 27, 1988 I received a collect call from my father. He was in custody and immediately started the conversation with his defense. He said, "Son, I'm in jail in Georgia. Do you remember when I told you about that guy that was threatening to kill your brother and sister if I didn't help him kidnap this woman? Do you remember what I am telling you son . . . I told you about it. Remember son?"

This call reminded me of the first time he called me from jail, except this time he was all business. I guess that shock value had worn off for him . . . and me. I remember exactly where I was sitting when he called and the mixed emotions that I felt at that moment. His defense was going to be that the other guy made him do it, and he wanted me to help him prove it.

But I was done helping my father. I was exhausted, sad, glad, numb and relieved all at the same time. I never did believe that he would come back with that money. Nothing he told me any more made sense or came true. I was relieved to have jail between my father and me again. It was a sick ending to the most intense year and a half of my life. He was finally back in custody after seventeen months of mayhem and revenge that cost four people their lives and showed me firsthand what hell looks like. This was a place I was ready to leave forever.

For me, that meant it was time to get busy burying memories again. I wasn't aware that this had become an art form for me, but apparently, I was very good at it. It would take some time, but I immediately began to close the trap door on these memories. It was time to enjoy myself, and I wasn't interested in having my father ruin my life anymore.

In order to enjoy myself, after all I had witnessed, I was going to need a reason to stick around until I would become willing to see the truth. God sent me a couple of Angels.

"There but for the grace of God go I . . ."

Chapter 6

A Game of Hide and Seek

At the end of my father's killing spree, I met my future wife for the first time. I had found a job as a sales manager in the travel industry at a popular nighttime entertainment complex where she worked. I am not sure how I pulled this off while my father was still on the loose, but I did. I really don't think I did this on my own because I was a wreck. I didn't believe in God at the time, but apparently God still believed in me because the next few years were incredible.

Shortly after we met, my father was arrested for the kidnapping and attempted murder of the drug dealer's wife. My wife did not meet my father while he was out and I didn't tell her about this, certainly not when it happened. The first time I told her about it was right before the news was about to break with the story of my father being charged in the diamond murder case. It took them over a year to charge him in that case, and it was a fluke that they figured it out. It didn't have anything to do with my call to CrimeLine, although police knew about the call. I was being interviewed by police about the case regularly, and I knew they were close to charging him.

The detective, Dan Nazerchuk, was very discrete about interviewing me, and I would sneak away from work, meet with detectives and head back to the office. This was how I lived, still being chased by this nightmare. It was strange to be at the office, head over to police headquarters, talk to police about my father's pending murder charge, and then go back to work. I was living a double life.

As for the interviews, I always let them know I thought my dad did it, but I was too afraid to tell them everything I knew. I had worked very hard to distance myself from this experience and was optimistic about my future for the first time in years. The thought of everyone finding out about what I knew and what I did was not worth the risk. I had just started a whole new life and I wasn't willing to give that up. Maybe it was selfish, but I didn't even want to *think* about what had happened to me any more, let alone start telling other people about it.

Nazerchuk knew that I had called CrimeLine, and he kept it under the radar. He was very gentle in taking me through questions, basically allowing me to indicate if he was right about something without making me say it outright. I trusted him, but not enough to open up completely, and I am certain that he knew that I knew more. He was very kind, and I was constantly debating what I should or should not tell him.

As much as I wanted to talk, I just couldn't do it. I had a new life, career, and girlfriend. I was not ready to jeopardize that. I tried to rationalize that they were going to get him without me anyway, and that was best for all. I had already paid my dues for this man. I wasn't about to volunteer myself to suffer more on his account. I tried not to think about the other families. I had my own problems to deal with, and it would be impossible to overcome them if I got all mixed up in this mess. That is what I told myself, anyway.

If I got involved and told the truth, how was I going to explain helping him burn that car? Damn, there was that car again, always lurking in the back of my mind. It was always there, right where my dad wanted it. The truth is, I couldn't even think about it without getting sick, let alone tell someone else about it.

Nazerchuk asked about the two black guys, but they still didn't know who they were or where they were from. They thought it was suspicious that the bodies were found in the same field as the diamond dealer, but I couldn't bring myself to tell them what I knew about that case either. Without their identities, I rationalized, it wouldn't do much good anyway.

I did, however, consistently suggest that they look at his long distance phone records and *implied* that I believed he did it. He used my long distance card for a few months after he got home, and I thought they might find something there, but that is as far as I would allow myself to go.

I was still terrified by the thought of him knowing that I had betrayed him, too. It makes no sense that I would still be afraid with him in jail, but I was. I have no explanation other than that is how I felt, and it wasn't a weak feeling. It was powerful.

I told my future wife about the Caruso murder, before the news was about to break, and she was relatively unfazed. This is a characteristic that became very important for the woman who would claim me as her husband. She came from a very loving family. Jokingly, I debate that with her sometimes, but it always comes back to *my family* . . . end of discussion.

Anyway, she and I had dated for several months when my father finally went on trial in Orlando for the Caruso murder. The trial was all over the news. I would nervously grab the newspaper each day, looking for the front page headline and wondering if anybody was going to figure it out. Some girl in my office made a connection with my last name one day, and she joked in front of the staff, "Hey this guy's name is Vining too. Is that your brother?" . . . I paused, looked at everyone, smiled and said with a laugh, "No that's my dad!" They all broke up laughing as I walked into my office.

There were certain characteristics that I had picked up from my dad. I could be very charming and sell almost any- thing, no matter how I felt inside. I learned to be cool under pressure, and this kind of pressure made me feel that I had power and control. I liked that I could do that.

Because my office was downtown, I would sneak over to the courthouse, sit in on the murder trial for a few hours, and then slip back to work. It was another weird time in my life. It felt like I was still connected to two different worlds. I was leaving one while returning to the other. I was returning to a life that I thought I had lost forever.

I was having some real success with my job and rela- tionships while still dealing with my past and that time I spent with my father. My emotions were all over the board, but mostly I felt like someone who had escaped a terrible fate. It felt like being narrowly missed by a runaway freight train, only the end of the train was still passing me on the tracks. It was like being aware of how close you just came with incredible relief, but still having a great deal of anxiety from the sound of the train as it went soaring past, not completely certain that you were out of danger yet.

My girlfriend's mother finally figured it out after reading the newspaper. Call it a woman's intuition or just plain good mothering, but she put two and two together and asked me about it at her house one afternoon. She just knew. Needless to say, my future in-laws were not excited about their daughter being with me. I never blamed them and felt that I would have done the same thing if my daughter were dating a guy whose dad was on trial for a high-profile murder. Eventually, however, they accepted me and welcomed me into their family—another point in my life when God was doing for me what I could not do for myself.

We married in 1992 and she was a stabilizing force in my life, like a rock, well, as stabilizing as you can be for a guy like me. She did a pretty good job of showing me how to be responsible. The only reason I had any success in my life was because of this woman. I focused on work and started to advance in my sales jobs to Director, then eventually to Vice President of Sales and Marketing of an entertainment company owned by Rank Leisure USA. Finally, at the age of thirty-two, it looked like I was getting my life together.

My wife became pregnant, and I started a business. I don't recommend telling your wife that you are planning on starting a new business while she is pregnant with your first child, and you have very little savings in the bank, but that is what I did. It was a small travel company, but it filled a need that no one else had addressed and turned out to be very successful.

Soon after that I started a non-profit association to market our destination, and this venture too, quickly became successful. I couldn't believe the success I was having. At one point I had thought I would never laugh again, but life was feeling pretty good.

This was a shock to my family and to those who knew anything at all about my background. They had no idea about the secret details of my experience with my dad, but they had seen enough to lower their expectations of me. My brothers and sisters were all struggling with drugs and other issues. I looked like a hero, a guy who rose above it all.

We then had a baby girl, and life was a dream—a good dream. My daughter was the most wonderful thing that ever happened to me. I knew I was going to be a great dad, nothing like my father. I heard it said that abused kids often turn into abusive parents, but I always knew I was going to be a good dad. I wanted to *be loved*, but more than that, I think, I wanted *to love*.

From the beginning I was involved in her life. I never missed anything, and I often volunteered at her school. I wanted to be around kids as much as possible. I still do. I would read to her class and join them on field trips. I was making up for my own lost childhood while participating in hers. My little girl revealed to me what pure unconditional love feels like. Life was good.

It seemed that there was nothing I couldn't do. I had gained a lot of weight after high school, and that became my next challenge to overcome. I lost almost fifty pounds, started running and wound up running a marathon in 2000. It was a slow time, but I did it. I celebrated my fortieth birthday on top of the world. Again, my friends and family were very impressed with all my accomplishments, and it seemed that I was unstoppable. I had overcome all the tragedy in my life to become a successful, self-made man. I was on top of the world, family, house, my own business, and able to do anything I set my mind to. Or so it seemed. I didn't know it at the time, but something was still missing.

Through all of this success and achievement, I thought I was healthy as a horse, but these aggravating physical issues kept popping up. Although I argued I was healthy, my wife knew something was up and didn't understand why I would deny that weird things kept happening with me. I call them aggravating, but the truth is they were sometimes paralyzing, such as migraine headaches that were completely debilitating. I would get one in the office and not be able to move. My wife would have to drive me home and put me in the bedroom with the blinds drawn.

I was having too much fun, or so I thought, to pay attention to this problem. I tried my best to ignore it and blow it off, but my old faithful behavior of denying things was beginning to fail me. These things were becoming increasingly more difficult to deny.

Most of the time, I felt invincible, but I was still drinking a lot. You see, I had this little issue with sometimes blacking out when I drank. I would wake up and not be able to remember the events from the night before. It was becoming a real problem. Now that I had a family, I really couldn't understand why I couldn't manage this behavior. This was not something new, though. I had been drinking that way from an early age. It was just harder to ignore and justify now that I had a wife and little girl at home. It seemed that I had everything I ever wanted and had climbed out of the pit of hell, but something just wasn't right. Why wasn't this enough?

I had never shared with anyone, not even my wife, what I knew about my dad. In fact, after a period of time, I no longer shared it with myself, at least not consciously. In the beginning, I would be sitting at a bar with friends and find myself drifting away into my past. I would look at them laughing and having fun, and I would wonder if any of them had any idea just how ugly this world really was. When I did that, I would begin to recall that sick feeling of separation that I so desperately wanted to escape. I didn't like the way it made me feel. Over time, I was able to stop doing it. It took a while, but eventually those thoughts faded away completely. Or so I thought.

Apparently these demons were still in me and they were about to become very active again. These secrets I had been keeping were about to return me to hell for another visit. Only this time I was the enemy.

Chapter 7

Deadly Mind Games—
Rundown by My Past

I was having all this success, but I just couldn't seem to sustain my happiness, because of physical problems. At first, I was able to ignore it and focus on all the fun I thought I was having. Although I didn't realize it at the time, these ailments had been plaguing me ever since my father went back to jail.

Early on, I would have pinkish red bumps spread all over the trunk of my body. The bumps looked like chinch bugs and would last a few days before disappearing, only to return again. I went to a doctor, and he couldn't tell me any thing about the rash other than it did not seem to be life threatening. This was the beginning of a pattern that would be repeated over and over.

The next thing I remember was having random episodes when my temperature would rise without warning. I would feel fine, having a good time, and suddenly my temperature would start to soar then I wouldn't feel so good any more, and I'd have to leave parties or events with very little explanation. It was weird, and I started checking my temperature fairly often when I felt this way. It would go up two or three degrees.

These episodes would last for only a few hours, and typically the next day my fever would be gone, just like that. Again I went to a doctor's office, and everyone seemed to think I was crazy. They had no explanation for this. Not only did they not have an explanation, but I was also getting the feeling that they didn't believe me.

Through all of this time I was having sleep problems and frequent nightmares. The most common sleep problem was sleep apnea, where I would wake up after I would stop breathing for a while. This was dangerous, and I would be gasping for air, frightened to death. This particular condition was usually accompanied by a nightmare where I was trying to wake myself up before I died. The dream was pure panic, and that feeling always carried over after waking suddenly.

Some of the physical problems were a little less menacing, such as random nose bleeds, more skin conditions, and severe allergies that would block my breathing almost completely. Then there were other problems that were becoming more serious and more threatening. It's almost as if something might be trying to bring me down, and if one problem didn't do the job another more serious problem was sent in its place. I had some issues as a kid, as well, but these were all new and constantly changing.

Shortly after I started my business, I remember having a good day, and then suddenly my vision began to give me problems. I couldn't seem to put a sentence together. I was scared to answer the phone because I could think the thought, but when I spoke, the words weren't in the right order. I would concentrate and try to say a specific sentence, but the words would come out all mixed up. I'd try to avoid human contact for a couple of hours until it passed, but this really scared me. This was also accompanied by a numb feeling in my hand. I remember trying to explain it to my wife and feeling like a complete idiot. How do you explain something like this? I may not have been connecting the dots, but my wife was. She was getting tired of my little problems because there was always something.

Eventually I started to have migraine headaches. I didn't know what they were at first, and I thought I had a brain tumor or something very serious. I was melodramatic anyway, so the health problems were giving me many opportunities to practice this. I began to think everything was life-threatening.

When the migraines happened, I couldn't move, almost paralyzed by the pain, so back to the doctor I went for tests. Finally, a diagnosis was given, or so it seemed. These problems were starting to add up. New issues began to pop up as the old ones, although less frequent, continued to flare up. This continued happening while I was successfully building my new business.

Through all of this I continued to drink, and the blackouts became a regular part of my drinking. There was alcoholism throughout my family. My mom and dad, my brother, and my grandmother all had drinking problems. I thought I was different. Again, no such luck.

My next two physical gifts were about to bring it all together for me in a place known to many as *desperation*. I began to experience serious and chronic back pain. I had been running a lot, which made me feel good and apparently helped to relieve some of the stress I was dealing with. The back pain was now taking that option away from me, only two years since I ran the marathon. This compounded my problems and for the first time since I met my wife, at age forty-two, I was becoming depressed. Here I was with a great life, overcoming all this crap, and now I couldn't even enjoy my wife and daughter. The guilt was overwhelming, and I began to take pain pills regularly.

After months on the pain pills, I realized I was addicted and fought my way off on my own. I was severely depressed, and my new-found love for life was gone. I was back to the place I was as a kid, hating myself for my failure again. I would ask myself how could I blow this gift of a new life, and why was all this being taken away from me?

Well, it was about to get worse. When I got off the pain pills, I was introduced to my new illness, irritable bowel syndrome. At first I thought it was just my digestive system adjusting to getting off the pain pills, but things kept getting worse. After two weeks of diarrhea (going ten to fifteen times a day) I finally went to the doctor, and although a diagnosis was given nothing could help me. Nothing worked, and I was like this for almost six months.

My wife was growing weary of these so-called issues and began to question whether or not they were real. How many times could she pick me up and help me get over one issue, only to have something else take its place? I was back in a nightmare again, and this time I was taking my family with me. These illnesses were becoming life-threatening, and the depression was killing me. The truth was: My Mind was *the one* killing me, and everything around me, including my family.

The depression was the worst thing because I just couldn't accept having to take medication for it. Not me. Remember, I had overcome all these terrible things, and for what? So I could throw my life away because I was *depressed*? The depression was real, though. It's hard to describe what it feels like not to care. It was a sick, numb feeling in my stomach. I didn't want to die, but I really didn't care about living either. I was back in no man's land.

Maybe it was my wife and daughter that I lived for, I don't know. I was tired all the time and I didn't have any energy for anything, even the things I once loved to do. It was horrifying, looking at a beautiful daughter like mine and feeling that I couldn't get excited about life anymore. It was a hopeless feeling.

After about six months I wound up back on the pain pills, and my back problems returned. The only upside to this was that my IBS was actually being treated by the amount of pain pills I was taking, which was becoming more and more. As I remember this, I can't help thinking about what I put my wife through. It was one thing after another until finally it all came together with major back surgery and an addiction to pain pills. Yes, I was about to add drug addict to my resume. Things were definitely going the wrong way again. That runaway train had returned, only this time I was the conductor, and I was dragging my family down the tracks with me. I didn't realize that what I was running from was inside of me.

A couple of months before surgery my wife gave me a book titled *The Divided Mind* by Dr. John Sarno. In this book he theorizes that Tension Myoneural Syndrome (TMS) is a defensive reaction of the mind to prevent expression of repressed rage and anxiety that manifests itself in many forms (all of which I had), but most notably, back pain.

At first I was insulted by the suggestion that all my suffering might be the result of some kind of mental issue. I told my wife I thought *she was the crazy one*, not me. I was the last guy in the world that would believe something as outrageous as this idea that all my trouble was all in my mind. I put the book aside, but she continued to nag me to at least read some of it. Finally, one day I picked it up and started reading just so I could tell her that I did it.

The book focused on the back pain but also identified many of the other illnesses and issues that I had been dealing with for years. I still didn't believe it, but that certainly got my attention. There were some workbook journaling exercises designed to help the reader take a closer look at his past. I started doing some of these exercises while I was at home, preparing for back surgery. It was interesting to say the least, but I wasn't at all convinced that these theories applied to my situation. I went through with the surgery to have a disk replaced in my lower back in April of 2004.

To this day, I am not sure if I needed that surgery, but my back has totally recovered. I had a wonderful surgeon, and my disk was degenerative, but we'll never know if that was responsible for the pain or not. Personally, I don't think it was. I finally found something I could point to as the culprit in all this, and I hung my hopes on that.

My wife has a sense about these things and one of the first questions she asked the doctor after surgery was to see the disk. This is not usually the first question asked after surgery, but my wife knew something was up (even though she couldn't put her finger on it). The doctor confirmed that it was damaged, but later admitted there is no way of knowing if the disc was the cause of all that pain. He simply had to trust me with that piece of the puzzle.

During these mostly wonderful years of my life, I had successfully deleted the most frightening memories of my time with my father from my consciousness. The conversation we had when he told me about killing the two black guys simply didn't pop up any more, at least not in thoughts and words. I never shared these stories with anyone, not even my wife or trusted friends. Now, these memories were trying to find another way out, and they would not be denied.

Four months from my surgery date, I finally accepted that I was addicted to the pain pills and became willing to ask for help. My back was no longer the problem, but I continued taking massive amounts of prescription drugs for pain, depression, anxiety and sleep. I was still not free. No matter what I did, I could not seem to outrun this dark cloud that had settled over my life. This, it turned out, would be a gift. It's called the Gift of Desperation.

I was done running.

I felt completely hopeless, alone, washed up and left for dead. Seeing my daughter and wife go about life while I was becoming a liability, addicted to pain pills, was like watching a movie from a prison cell—a movie about me harming my family. I couldn't save them from me. I could only watch as I slowly destroyed their lives. I was tired of being in prison.

This is when the most important words I ever thought or said came through: *"God, if you really are there, please help me."* I had said them before, but this time I meant them. I went to a small Adoration Chapel, got on my knees, looked up at the stained glass image of Jesus Christ with the inscription: *Jesus, I Trust in You*, and I said those words: "God, if you really are there, please help me."

I didn't expect anything to work, but I was out of options. I needed help, and so far, no human power was able give me what I was searching for. I had tried doctors, therapists, self-help books, you name it. None of it worked. I had pictures of my daughter all around me to give me the strength to live, and I couldn't look at them any more because of how I was letting her down. God was the only hope left, and I thought it was a long shot at best. It was the last place I went for help.

The sun was shining though the stained glass, and it looked beautiful. Maybe there was a glimmer of hope, after all. I didn't just say it once and move on. It was more like begging. I figured if this God thing was real, I had some explaining to do. There was going to be hell to pay.

I had no idea that it would work because I had never had a relationship with a higher power—or even believed that it was possible. It seemed to me to be the last door at the end of a long, torturous, lonely hallway. Apparently, God was listening.

Chapter 8

Glimpses of Heaven—
Finding a New Freedom

The experience I am about to share with you is one that would have caused me to make fun of other people. I know what it feels like to be on the other side as an agnostic or nonbeliever. In fact, the old me would have dismissed this story as delusional thinking and weakness. I would have read this and dismissed the author as probably too weak to face life on life's terms, as someone who instead must believe in something that cannot be proven.

My miracle happened only a few days after I went through a fairly violent, rapid detox process for my pain pill addiction. I checked into the facility on August 25, 2004, and was released after two nights and three days on August 27. That Sunday we were in church, and I was a physical and mental wreck.

I didn't want to go to church, but my wife had had enough of dealing with all my issues. This detox procedure cost a lot of money, and she wasn't interested in me not participating in life any more. Even though I felt awful I went. I felt as if everything inside of me, including my brain and muscles, had been mixed up in a giant blender and poured back inside my body.

Our church had a small choir, and the music is not the focal point of the service, but when the melody started my entire body and soul lit up with an indescribable rush of energy. We were sitting in the front row and as emotions began to overflow, the tears came rushing out. I cried uncontrollably, but it was the most incredible feeling I have ever had in my life.

Nothing even comes close.

It felt like the music was being played by angels, with violin sounds and beautiful singing all in perfect harmony. I don't remember what our pastor was saying other than he was part of the whole, and everything flowed beautifully with what I was experiencing.

This next part may seem odd, but this is what I felt, and I'll try to describe the sensation. This feeling or experience was felt, not thought, and it happened while I was still completely connected to what was happening in the church. I don't know if that makes sense, but it wasn't as if I drifted off in a day-dream. I was completely present.

The sensation I had was of being in a beautiful long Cadillac convertible traveling effortlessly on an open road. I was not driving but completely connected to the experience, and it was absolutely exhilarating. It was a warm, breezy and comforting feeling. The overriding emotion was that I was safe, with the most notable characteristic being the complete absence of fear. What happened next is more than I ever expected and something I simply didn't believe happened to people.

With the fullness of the music, singing, vibrant lights of the church and the feeling of moving effortlessly down an open road, I felt a loving and gentle presence on my shoulder. It was the clearest feeling I had ever known—again . . . this was not perceived in words, but as a feeling. The feeling was powerful, overwhelming and quite clear. It simply expressed this thought into my soul: *I've been with you all along, you were always safe.* I felt completely safe at that moment and had an awareness that I had never really been alone, ever. I cried uncontrollably, and it felt wonderful.

I knew what this was when I felt it. It was an undeniable feeling of connectedness, connected to something that expressed pure love. No drug or experience in my life had ever produced anything like this. It was distinctive in nature, but more importantly, clear in what it communicated to me . . . in me and through me.

As for the imagery of the Cadillac, I don't know why it came through that way, but I can say that some of my greatest fears were experienced while in that Cadillac with my father. I always felt trapped in that car. I first learned of his plan to kill people in that car, and I burned that car with him the day after I tried to turn him into police.

That was when I realized that my dad and I were enemies, and he was an enemy I had no business messing with. I was out of my league. That morning was one of the most terrifying moments of my life. A lot of my fear was identified with that Cadillac. As it turned out, my father was the one who was out of his league because I was being protected by my *real* Father. That was the message of that day in church, loud and clear.

"I've been with you all along . . . you were always safe."

Afterward, I began to wonder if the message were real or if I had imagined it. The more time passed, the less powerful it seemed. I wanted to relive the feeling, but just couldn't get there.

It was very similar to the feeling of peace *beyond words* that I had experienced after my mother's funeral. Back then, I had no faith in a higher power that I was aware of, and it was easy for me to dismiss it as a fantasy and shake it off.

But this time it came on the heels of my visit to the Adoration Chapel and my call for help. It just seemed that there were a lot of coincidences happening in my life since I made that simple prayer—too many to dismiss as fantasy without a closer look, and I started searching for answers.

As I began to explore this strange new world, I was confronted with some of my old perceptions about the possibility of an experience like this. When I was having some success on what can only be described as self-will, I had a few standard lines for conversations with people who said they believed in God:

No one ever found God on the way to the prom.
I made this statement to emphasize that God was always found
in weakness, not in victory or success as I understood it. To
me, this clearly showed that people who "found God" were
weak themselves, and God was a crutch and a cop out.

*Okay, let me get this straight, you believe God moved all
these events around for your benefit?*
I was all about coincidences and making fun of people who
believed in them. Imagine the irony in that. I loved trying to
"pop people's bubble" when they took delight in coincidences
that they considered God-engineered events in their lives.

And my favorite line about God?
*If there is a God, don't you think he'd like to know where
HE came from?*
This was one of my favorite lines because people generally
didn't have a quick or reasonable answer to this. I took great
joy in trying to shut down a conversation with this sarcastic
line.

After that experience I had in church, I began to rethink my
position on these questions. In another one of those events
that I used to call coincidences, I picked up a spiritual book in
a book store and bought it without a recommendation or
researching the book first. I don't ever remember having
bought a book without researching it first. It just caught my
eye.

The subject matter was an interpretation of the teachings
of Jesus. In the book the author wrote about these types of
spiritual experiences, and mine was a common reaction to them.
The book stated that people do one of two things when a
spiritual experience like this happens. They either begin to talk
themselves out of it and dismiss it as an illusion or fantasy or

they begin to pursue it, to feel it and know it again. I began to do the latter.

It would be a while before I would experience anything close to that feeling again, but now I had the advantage of knowing that there was a Higher Power with me because the message wasn't past tense. The message was here, and it was now. The feeling I experienced had expressed: *I've been with you all along.* That was my first real tangible spiritual marker, and I didn't care how far it was to the next one because I now believed that it was real. I also believed that this gentle hand had been on me even in the darkness of doubt when I couldn't feel it. I wanted to understand just how that could be.

As for the so-called "clever comments" I used to make:

No one ever found God on the way to the prom.

This was simple to answer because of what I have learned about The Truth. The statement is true, generally speaking, but the point I was trying to make was way off base. People who have material success and are finding happiness in temporary things seem to have a harder time of finding true peace than those who are desperate. Material things, although temporary, do bring about a similar feeling of peace and joy, but it's nothing compared to the real thing. The real peace that can be found through a Higher Power is more rewarding than all the gold in the world. Desperation seems to open up the possibility for help and a willingness to look for peace elsewhere, which turns out to be the right place to look.

Today I understand all this confusing talk about giving up material things for God, and I see what that means to me now. It is not necessarily to be taken literally, although some of us have to experience that before we can let go. The satisfaction from these things is similar on a much smaller scale to the feelings of true peace and happiness that we can find in ourselves, through God. Therefore, if we are getting this feeling from material things, we are less likely to look elsewhere. We feel a false sense of security, and it becomes a blocker. The problem is that the material things are always temporary in nature, and we have no control over these things. Material things will always come and go in our lives, making the pursuit of them as our primary purpose a mistake because that often blocks us from the real treasure and true peace.

I do not mean that we must live in poverty to be happy. That mistake may deceive someone into thinking they do not want to pursue true peace because it might require giving up material success. The truth is we can have that kind of prosperity as well, but to have the real peace we all seek, spiritual success must precede it. Desperation often opens up this door to a new way a living. Another book that I began to study apparently already had this all figured out.

> Blessed are the poor in spirit: for theirs is the
> kingdom of heaven.
> —Matthew 5:3

Okay, let me get this straight, you believe God moved all these events around for your benefit?
This one is fun for me. You see I really went out of my way to show people just how smart I was by dissecting the absurdity of this explanation. In fact, I used this to reinforce my own belief that these events were not God-engineered. It was almost like a defense mechanism.

I believe all of us have times throughout our lives when we feel something greater than ourselves engineering opportunities for us with unexpected help, chance meetings and shocking resolutions to previously unsolvable problems. At the time these circumstances feel extraordinary, but as time passes, we seem to forget.

As for this question, like so many others, I don't have all the answers yet. The simple answer seems to be that God does not move all these events around for our personal entertainment, but when we are in the right place at the right time and paying attention we are moving in God's plan. When we do this, we see glimpses of it. It is not about God moving everything for us, but it is about us standing in the right spot to see mysterious glimpses of God. Some of these experiences are quite possibly engineered to help increase our faith as we make our journey towards a deeper understanding of divine wisdom.

The more I am present and looking for them, the more I experience these moments. The humor in all this is that my life is so filled with *coincidences* now that I dedicated an entire chapter of this book to revealing them. It offers proof of how insane my previous explanation of these events was, before my recovery. God has given me more than enough experiences with miracles to offer up an amends for my old behavior! Just another coincidence?

If there is a God, don't you think he'd like to know where HE came from?

This one's a little tougher. In fact, I don't have an answer that solves this question, but I do know this: There are two *qualities of God* that we cannot comprehend nor understand, and they are *infinity* and *eternity*. At least I can't. No matter how hard I think about what these mean, I still come up blank. I would place this question in the category of something we just don't have the capacity to understand.

The Pursuit of the Truth

Since my search didn't start *on the way to the prom*, I had a dilemma. Everything that I knew or thought about a dependence on God or a life of *doing God's will* was viewed as a weakness. The only reason I was really considering such a belief was because I was desperate. For starters, that sounded a lot like weakness to me. I had risen above all this evil only to fall victim to my own missteps: what was I going to do now?

Fortunately, I had that wonderful spiritual experience to rely upon, but over time it became distant, and at times, it didn't seem so important. It wasn't enough to keep me convinced that there was a higher power that I could rely upon. As for the phrases *rely upon* and *doing God's will*, I had some problems with them too.

First and most importantly, I just didn't see how a Higher Power would be interested in me having fun or being happy. This sounded more like work, or worse yet, giving up on the best life has to offer. My image of doing God's will was always of being sent alone to Africa to work in the heat and help diseased sick people. Some people might enjoy that, but it didn't sound like fun to me. That's not a joke. It's the kind of life I was expecting if I tried this. So that gives you an idea of just how desperate I was, because it was suddenly worth the risk. I loved my family, but if I had to go to Africa to keep from going back to that nightmare I had been living, I was going. *Sorry girls, I'm packing my robe and sandals and headed to Africa, thanks for all you did for me.*

Two other issues I had with this situation right up front was all this talk about God may not always give you what you want, but you will always get what you need. This sounded bad from top to bottom. My thinking at the time was: W*hy would I do anything that won't get me what I wanted?* As for getting only what I needed, that sounded like punishment, pure and simple. It sounded to me like *wanting* a candlelight dinner with Filet Mignon, Caesar Salad, Baked Potato and Chocolate Soufflé— but instead, getting military rations of canned beans and franks with a moon pie.

Finally, I had a concern about the teaching that *God had to come before material things,* or more accurately, that we had *to let go of these things for a true spiritual life.* This one seemed nonnegotiable, and I wasn't willing to do that so I came to this compromise . . .

I'm going to go for it, but still keep my material possessions. I was also pretty sure that I wasn't going to move to Africa if asked, and I'd still try to get what I wanted, but besides that, I was in.

No ego here, right? I'm going to this for you, God, but I'm going to do it my way, okay? The good news for me was God has a sense of humor, too, and didn't hold this against me. One key ingredient apparently overrode every one of those things . . . willingness. That's all I needed, willingness and a simple desire to seek the Truth.

The first and most important step for me was an awareness of how the ego worked and how to recognize it. I found this information in the Twelve-Steps of the Anonymous programs, as a gift being passed on from others who had similar experiences in their lives. This is where my recovery started. I will not use a lot of space to cover this other than to say that the twelve steps are all about a spiritual awakening, and it is here that I found my way. It is a spiritual fellowship of men and women who help each other along the path to experience their own spiritual relationship. It is the most wonderful fellowship that I am aware of.

There is where I saw proof for the first time that God was real. It's very simple really. Most of our fellowship come to twelve-step programs of recovery with a problem that no human power could help us to solve. Only when we cleaned house and learned to trust God were we saved. The trusting in God was accomplished through working the steps and the sharing of others, which results in a belief in a higher power based on fact, not fiction. It is here that I saw God's work first-hand and decided it was worth taking the trip. The return of my memories was a result of these steps and it saved my life, or more accurately, gave me a new one. This new life came with a promise that I could be Happy, Joyous and Free regardless of the circumstances in my life. Now that got my attention. The bottom line is: Happiness is all I ever really wanted, that is what I have been seeking my whole life.

This process required willingness, courage and endurance,

but others showed me the way. I began to first clear away the wreckage of my past through journaling and deep self-exploration. I went back to my notes from the journaling that I did just before my surgery and started there.

Maybe it was merely a coincidence that my wife handed me that book only a few months before I was brought to my knees. You remember the book, right? It was the one that led me to tell my wife that I thought that *she* was crazy?

I was about to find all those deep dark secrets that I had been hiding from for all those years. What I was about to uncover was going to turn my whole world upside down, including my entire belief system. The insanity of it all was about to be exposed to the light of day. It was time to take an axe to that trap door of shame.

Chapter 9

Shine a Light—Lost Memories
of a Cold-Blooded Killer

Wednesday, November 17, 2004

I was on my knees in the family room of our home. It was about five A.M., and I was reflecting on some journaling that I had been doing for the past few months. The night before, as suggested, I shared my life story with someone in recovery that I had come to trust.

I had been off of the pills for three months, and now I was *cleaning house* so that it wouldn't happen again. These particular steps in this process ask that we "make a searching and fearless moral personal inventory of ourselves," then "admit to God, to ourselves, and to another human being the exact nature of our wrongs."

I went through my life story with my friend and identified that my father was on Death Row, my mom was an alcoholic and that my stepmother had abused me. The list also contained a lot of other fears and resentments from my past, but that was all I said about my dad. I told my friend that he killed a woman, I knew it and that I had accepted it.

Most people describe the feeling after this step in recovery as euphoric, but that was not my experience. I felt unsettled and uneasy after that night. It was suggested that I go home and quietly think through everything that I had written down and shared about my past memories to be sure that I covered everything. I waited until morning to do this.

The next morning I was kneeling comfortably on my living room floor reflecting on everything that I had shared the night before. Suddenly I was flooded with the memories from that night at Applebee's Restaurant. It hit me like a freight train. The moment that memory returned to me, it was complete and vivid in every detail, as if it were the day after it happened.

My initial thought, as fear began to grip my entire being, was *Oh My God*. I said this to myself over and over again. I began to tremble as I went through *the tape*. There were so many emotions that I still cannot put it into words. This was one of my darkest secrets and it was buried deep inside of me. I spent years burying this secret so that it would never see the light of day. Now here it was again. I was trembling, alone in my living room. I was overwhelmed with fear . . . and full of shame.

I again felt sick, but this was a different kind of sick. This was the kind of sickness that comes from shame. I was wondering if somehow I could have protected people from being murdered, but did nothing. I didn't understand the timeline of what happened or when and if this knowledge could have stopped my father along the way.

I left the house and went for a long walk. It was still dark out, but the peace of meditation had long since left me and been replaced by a racing mind. Everything kept coming back to one question. Could I have prevented my father from killing Georgia Caruso? When did I know what I knew, and what did I do about it? I remembered the call to CrimeLine, but could I have done more? *Was her death my fault?*

As I wrestled with these questions, I began to think about what to do next. This feeling of blaming myself for something that my father had done was the reason I ran from this responsibility in the first place. It was the reason that I could not live with this memory. This time I didn't have to think about it. I was being offered a second chance. Intuitively I knew what I was supposed to do next.

I came home and walked into the bathroom dressing area, where my wife was getting ready for work. I sat down and said, "There is something I need to tell you." I paused as I gathered my thoughts and summoned the courage to let it out. "My dad killed two other guys, and I know about it. I don't just know about it, I know everything about it."

Instead of shock, she looked relieved. Yes, relieved. The next words out of her mouth surprised me. She said, "I knew it! I knew there was something bugging you." We had been married for thirteen years, and she had witnessed my struggle with all of those physical and emotional illnesses. She always suspected that these issues were caused by something "mental". She found relief in this revelation.

We discussed my options, but the decision was already made. She wasn't quite ready to agree with that decision, but she knew she had to support what I needed to do. It wasn't as though I thought of this as a second chance at the time. There was a purpose to all this that was guiding me. I just knew what I was supposed to do.

I had to put the feelings of what I did or didn't do aside and just do the right thing. What happened in the past had nothing to do with what I needed to do now. It had been seventeen years, and my father was already on Death Row, but the right thing to do was to call the police and tell them my story. I didn't need any more time to think about it, only to consider who I would call.

I picked up the phone and called homicide detective Dan Nazerchuk. He was the investigator who had handled that case and solved that crime. It was Nazerchuk that brought the murder charge that sent my father to Death Row in 1990. I had come to trust him during the investigation and thought he was a compassionate guy. He questioned me several times during that time and treated me with care and understanding. I always felt that Nazerchuk knew that I was cornered in this whole mess. As odd as it was, I considered him a safe haven. I liked being in his presence. I wanted him to be successful in prosecuting my father, and I know he sensed it. There was a connection between us. He knew that I could not encourage him openly, but I am sure he sensed that I thought of him as one of the good guys.

I had a DUI a couple of days after the trial when my father was sentenced to die in Florida's electric chair. It was Nazerchuk who showed up to tell the judge that I had been through a lot, and if there was ever a case where someone deserved a break, this was it. He didn't ask for special favors. He only asked the judge to consider the circumstances that I was dealing with. The judge held me accountable, but he was extremely fair and lenient. I really needed that break, and I was grateful for his help.

My memory of the murders came back to me on a Wednesday. On Saturday morning I called information and got Dan Nazerchuk's home phone number. It was a beautiful morning, and I stood outside my house to call him. His familiar voice answered the phone, and I immediately felt that I was doing the right thing. I asked if he remembered me, and he said of course.

I asked if he remembered questioning me about the two black guys during the Caruso investigation, and he answered, "Yes." Then I said, "Well, I know all about it. Everything." Then I told him the story. I also apologized for not telling him the truth all those years ago. He said he completely understood why I did what I did. That helped to release me a little bit more from the self-imposed guilt that I had attached to this event.

As always, he was warm and friendly. He said he'd follow up with cold case detectives on Monday and that he'd have them call me. They did, and we set an appointment date.

On December 1, 2004, I met Dan Nazerchuk at the police headquarters building. We hugged and talked briefly. He was happy to hear that I had a family of my own. He then took me upstairs and introduced me to cold case detectives Lee Allen and Duwana Pelton. They had the case file on the desk in a conference room with a tape recorder. They were pleasant, but it was obvious that they were skeptical. I am sure that they were looking at me as a possible suspect with what I was about to tell them.

Once the formality of our greeting was over, Nazerchuk put his hand on my shoulder and said to the other detectives, "You can trust anything he tells you." Then he left and they asked me to tell my story. I told them every detail exactly the way I remembered it. When I was finished, I could see the astonishment in their faces. I could tell they now trusted me and believed my story.

I asked them if I had described the case that was in the file folder sitting on the table, and they simply said, "To a 'T'." They said that I had just described the murder scene in perfect detail. They then told me with complete fascination that they had been given the names of the two suspects' just days before I called. They said, "We have never had anything like this happen in twenty years of working cold cases, not even close."

I was incredibly relieved when I left there that day, but I knew I wasn't done with this. They had asked me if I was prepared for what my dad's defense might be, then suggested that he might try to say that I did it. He might suggest that I certainly knew an awful lot about a murder scene for someone who had not been there.

I decided right then that *this confession* would be much more effective if it were in his words instead of mine. I simply needed to come up with a plan to get my father to talk. The tables were suddenly turned. It was my turn to con him and give him that familiar *can't rationalize this feeling* experience that he had given me so freely while he was murdering people.

This would be the beginning of an extraordinary journey through the past, one that would uncover all kinds of secrets— including lost memories, most buried deep inside me from as far back as I could remember. Suddenly, I began to understand everything. As I began to recount my father's behavior and crimes, from his killing spree to my childhood, I also began to learn about sociopaths. It was frightening and liberating at the same time.

I still wasn't ready to see the whole picture, though. This would take time. Sometimes the truth can be freeing and frightening at the same time. The truth was that I was close to my father, too close. I had a window into his soul and was afraid that if I looked too closely, I'd find myself there.

That is exactly what happened. What kept me going through this were glimpses of God's work all around me. They were like sign posts that pointed the way. Sometimes they were subtle, and at other times they were not so subtle. But always, they were there.

Chapter 10

God's Fingerprints on a Miracle that Collapses Time

Miracles are a way of earning release from fear. The miracle abolishes time. They undo the past in the present and thus release the future.

—A Course In Miracles

May, 2004—Storm Season

It is my belief that this road to recovery all started with a simple prayer. "God please help me." I had become addicted to pain pills, I had some health problems and my life had become unmanageable. The best part of this simple prayer—and one of the reasons I think it worked—was that I was desperate. I have since learned that God does his best work in my life when I don't have a pre-conceived path for him to follow, and in this case I was out of suggestions and just hopeless. I wish I could tell you that I had enough faith in God to say this prayer once and get on with my life, but that's not how it happened.

I had the surgery on my back and was recovered physically, but I couldn't get off the pain pills. This was a nightmare that only an alcoholic or addict can relate to. Anyway, I was in need of help and I knew it. That is the one thing I had going for me. I knew I needed help.

During this same period of time, my brother, who lived three hundred miles from me and had been in and out of recovery for years, was also repeating this same prayer. He had become addicted to Methadone, also a pain killer, and was now a full-blown junkie. One night he picked up the bottle again, got drunk and wrecked his car. He went to jail that night, and because of his record, had no chance of getting out for a while.

Some time went by before I finally learned that he was in jail. He had decided not to contact me this time, and his plan was to get out, drive to California and kill himself. His fantasy was to go out like Jim Morrison of The Doors.

Over the years I had a great deal of disappointment with my family and was considering giving up on my brother. I had bailed him out before, and he always let me down, but after discussing this with my wife, we decided to give him one last chance. She was really the influence behind this decision. She wanted to help him. What she didn't realize was that she was about to provide me with a valuable key to my past. It was I that she was about to set free.

I didn't trust my brother, but for some reason my wife and I decided to open our home to him. We invited him to move in with us while he got his act together after serving the time he had left to finish in jail. I wrote a letter to my brother while he was in jail, and he accepted our help. He decided to give sobriety one last chance.

He came to Orlando in July before the most incredible hurricane season on record. We had three major hurricanes come through Orlando the first two months that my brother lived with us. He often said these storms followed him, and I was beginning to believe him.

My brother's presence in my home helped me to understand how to get help for my pain pill addiction, and I entered into the rapid detox facility on August 25, 2004. I do not believe I would have done this had he not been there. My hospital visit was sandwiched between two of the hurricanes, Charley on August 13 and Frances on September 5. Another major hurricane, Jeanne, would hit Orlando September 25, but the real storm was brewing within me. That storm led up to a flood of memories about my father that were about to change the course of my life—and explain so many things in my past.

It was more than a coincidence that these events led us on a collision course such that we got help within three months of each other. We had lived in different towns and under completely different circumstances our entire lives. We had stayed in touch, but we had been separated since we were teenagers. The odds were against our getting help together, and while that was indeed interesting, it certainly didn't qualify as a miracle. It was other events that would cause me to take a much closer look at the bigger picture. There was another timeline developing here that would be much more revealing. In fact, it's beyond any worldly explanation.

My brother and I began to talk about our father, something we had not done in years. We would spend time together telling stories about our experiences with Dad and discussing how we felt about him. My brother's presence in Orlando and my desire to clear away the wreckage of the past led us to have conversations that started the healing process. No doubt, my brother was brought here for a reason.

A Prayer Brings Two Worlds Together.

On the night of November 16, I spent the evening with someone I trusted, sharing about my past and my deepest darkest secrets, fears and resentments. The next morning I sat quietly in meditation, going over the previous night. That is when the memories of this event came rushing back to me. The morning of November 17, 2004 is the day I recovered these memories.

Just a few miles from my house, the *same day* I was discovering these memories, cold case detectives received a break in the case from one of the victim's family members. In a separate incident in Washington D.C., a family member stumbled across the Florida Unidentified Decedents Database, a medical examiners website created to help relatives find the missing and presumed-dead.

He was searching for clues about his uncles who had vanished in Central Florida in the late 1980s. The relative thought that the pictures from the reconstructed remains looked like his uncles. He contacted the website operators and gave them the names of his missing uncles. This information was given to the medical examiner's office, and they contacted detective Duwana Pelton.

The call from the medical examiner's office was made to cold case detectives on November 17, 2004. After seventeen years this call took place the same day I recovered these memories. Two entirely separate events that were both needed to solve a seventeen-year-old case happened on the same day—after all that time. It also happened to be the day before the seventeenth anniversary of the murder of Georgia Caruso.

Detectives received the names of the unidentified victims and pulled the old file. The file was already sitting on the desk when retired Detective Dan Nazerchuk called to set the appointment for me to see them. It sounded too incredible to be possible that his call was related to the same case.

Skeletons Found *and* Identified.

Nazerchuk set the appointment with cold case detectives for December 1, 2004. It wasn't until later, when I was researching old newspaper articles about the case, that I realized the bodies had been found on the same day, December 1, 1987, exactly seventeen years earlier. I remembered reading that article at the time. I was hoping beyond hope that all this evil would just go away, but there it was in the newspaper for everyone to see.

Until that article on December 1, 1987, I didn't have enough information to give police. The day I saw it, I knew everything had changed. My conscience was pulling at me to do something, but I was still too terrified. All those years I had thought my failure to call the police is what allowed Georgia

Caruso to become murder victim number four. I was always too scared to look at the details of what happened because I thought I could have done more.

It wasn't until this all came out that I realized she was murdered *before* this article ran in the paper. Even if I had given them my father's name in connection with the newspaper article, there was still no other evidence, and the bodies would have remained unidentified. Finally, after the experience with CrimeLine, I didn't have any faith in the system. I did the best I could, given the circumstances.

These so-called coincidences have helped to free me from the unnecessary guilt and shame that I had been using to blackmail myself. Had these events not happened this way, I am not sure that I would have tracked down that old article to find that date. I became very interested in the dates surrounding the events because I had never heard of anything like this happening before.

This miracle seemed to alter the order of things. At first, it appeared to go back in time, but it actually went forward. It undid the past in the present, and in doing so, released the future. That, I believe, was its intended purpose for all concerned. I didn't understand it at the time, but its real function was not so much *for* me, but done through me for the benefit of others. In this case, it was the families of the victims that had their prayers answered. It turned out to be a natural spiritual expression of total forgiveness.

Miracles inspire gratitude and are faith-confirming. These events gave me the courage that I needed to look more closely at my past. Whenever the doubt began to creep back in, I would think about these events and remind myself that something much greater than me was guiding me.

These experiences are personal and the feelings of connectedness are very difficult to describe, but we all have them. Many people dismiss the feelings as crazy or tell themselves that it wasn't important, just a coincidence. Especially if the unexpected, yet coordinated events seem trivial at the time.

The good news about these particular events for me was that they were not trivial by any means.

The cold case detectives were also surprised when I met with them and told them the details of the double murder case that they had just pulled out. They said that my showing up after seventeen years to volunteer this information was extremely unusual, but it was not unheard of. They then went on to say that adding in the fact that the other family contacted the medical examiner's office with the names two weeks prior to my giving them the details of the crime made it unprecedented. What they unknowingly had witnessed was a correction of the past that collapsed time, effectively replacing the fear in me with gratitude.

Now armed with new-found confidence that something greater than me was at work, I knew it was time to bring my father back into the loop. My dad had been on Death Row for fifteen years when all this started to come back to me, and now it was time for me to pay him a visit and get him to talk about these murders again.

In order to do this, I needed to take a page from my father's very own playbook and create a con of my own. I was about to turn the tables on him; it was my turn to play conman. It was his turn to experience that uneasy feeling as the truth slowly and painfully revealed to him that I was not the man he thought I was, either.

I had learned to "act natural" around my father under extreme pressure, and now that skill was about to be put to the test. I was headed to Death Row with a couple of homicide detectives who would set up in a hidden room while I met my father with a surprise visit and a wire.

That's not all I had, though. This time I put my Faith in God.

Chapter 11

A Confrontation with Evil on Death Row

I had visited my father on Death Row before, but this trip was different. I was traveling to Union Correctional Institution with two homicide detectives and I intended to record a conversation with my father about two murders he had described to me years earlier.

The drive up to Death Row was a two hour trip from Orlando. The detectives were kind and compassionate, and I felt comfortable in their care. We talked a lot about sociopaths and how much damage they do to their families. They mentioned that the families of sociopaths (perpetrators) are often the forgotten ones, so to speak. Most of the attention in our society is about what damage is done to the victim's family, but there are two sides, as many of us know all too well.

The whole trip was surreal as my past and the present collided in front of an impersonal audience of strangers. I always thought that my relationship with my father was personal, but for the first time I understood that what my father did, and what I was a part of, was so heinous and touched so many other lives that it now belonged to the public. It was never my secret to keep. These are not family secrets that happened behind closed doors, but extremely invasive and offensive crimes to all of society.

I had thought a lot about my role in this situation and wondered what others might think of me, especially my family and friends who had known me all these years. Would they change their feelings about me once they learned that I was so close to this madness and appeared to do nothing to stop it? Would they consider me a part of it or sympathize with me as an innocent victim? These thoughts were leading me to the bigger question that was on my mind. Could I live with myself now after asking myself these same probing questions? Was I victim or participant?

Facing my father with detectives in a hidden room was going to be scary enough. I was incapable of debating these other issues and conflicts within myself while facing my dad at the same time, and I had to let it go. I was learning about "one day at a time", and that is exactly how I approached this day— no past, no future, just the present moment. On the way up I was very calm. I prayed a great deal about this day, and I spent quiet time early in the morning before leaving the house. The thought of facing my father and trying to get him to talk about these murders was frightening, and I knew it was something I could not do on my own. It is interesting that I can often find the greatest peace when I recognize circumstances are well beyond my control, and I am able to surrender the outcome to a higher power. That is what I did before I left the house.

As I have mentioned before, I idolized my dad when I was growing up and still continued to communicate with him. Occasionally, (every few years), I visited him on Death Row, and I would also write to tell him about my accomplishments, still looking for his approval even after all he had done. This is the most baffling part of all. I can't explain the mixed emotions, I can only share my experience. It was almost as if I completely compartmentalized things. On the one hand he was still my father, but on the other he was a cold-blooded killer.

I had been to Death Row before, and it is a creepy place to visit. It is impossible for me to go there without trying to feel what the prisoners feel. I don't know if it's just morbid curiosity, the way I think or because it's my dad, but it sends a chill up my spine and I can feel a heavy weight on me as I enter this world of pain and punishment. This place has a vibe to it. I don't like it, but in some ways it was attractive to me. As if I were watching a horrible accident or drawn to the sickness of it all.

The sounds of heavy metal doors open and close as you pass through. As you go deeper and deeper into this hell hole, everything feels indescribable. It slows down here, as if you are in a horror movie where bad is all around you, just beyond the shadows, and it is palpable. The cold damp walls have a smell and a feel to them as if the concrete were absorbing the sweat of the inmates. This is an unforgiving and serious place.

On this visit they brought us through the prison quickly and took me to a private room deep inside. There they prepped me with some suggestions for my behavior and placed a wire on me. I wasn't paying attention to their direction on how to act. Even though we were being recorded, this part was personal. It was unfinished business between me and good old Dad. I was ready, and this time I was the one going for the kill. I didn't care about the cops any more: it was time to face this.

I was moved to a small private room that is used for inmates to meet with their lawyers. The room was hard and cold, like the rest of this place, with one large thick glass window. The window was for the guards to see. There was a small rectangular table in the middle of the room with one chair on each side. Another recorder was placed under my chair, and then they sent for my father. He did not know I was coming, and I wasn't sure how he would react to me being in this "special" room, but again, I put my faith in another Father that I was learning to rely upon. I didn't concern myself with worry or circumstances. I simply stayed focused and calm.

I could hear his voice as he was coming down the hallway in chains and leg irons. They shackle all Death Row inmates when they are moving them in the prison. They also lock down all the other inmates. I watched through the glass window as he passed by to enter the room. He was wearing a bright orange prison uniform, his wrists were handcuffed to a wide leather belt around his waist, and he was sliding his feet to move. He seemed very adept at the sliding motion required to move with leg irons and chains around his ankles.

He entered the room. The guard removed the chains and shackles, but the handcuffs were left on. I could feel the bizarre nature of the relationship between these two men as they interacted. There was mutual respect, but only for the situation, not for each other. I could somehow feel that both men knew what would happen if the roles between these two men were suddenly reversed. One man's fantasy would become another man's worst nightmare.

The guard placed my dad directly across the table from me before leaving the room and closing the door. As I watched my father, I couldn't help but notice how much older and thinner he looked. He looked like such a small man. He was the same height, five feet, eight inches, but my memory of him was much larger. It's funny how the mind plays tricks on us like that. His hair had also grayed and thinned, and he didn't move with the same authority as he once did. This was what fifteen years on Death Row will do to a man, I thought. Even though he looked old and small I still had that awareness that he was lethal. In fact, he used his "meekness" to his advantage in disarming his victims before taking their very lives, and I knew he still had it in him. Just as I had trained myself to do when he exposed me to his killing spree all those years ago, I quickly dismissed the thought and relaxed. I was back in familiar territory.

I had entered the lion's den and I was about to do something to my father that was worse than anything he had ever known. I was his favorite son, the one he was always proudest of. He had introduced me to the guard by saying, "This is my boy, he's going to help me get out of here." This visit was about betrayal. For him it would be about a son betraying his father. For me it was about making right a father's betrayal of his own son.

He was shocked to see me, but also excited. It reminded

me of how he had conned so many of his victims. He would make them feel so excited about a deal that they failed to look at or recognize things that they should have been paying attention to. Meetings like this didn't happen unless you were a lawyer, but I had written to him that I had met with a powerful organization that was out to get bad cops, regardless of whether they thought the person committed the crime. He had always said that the police in his case fabricated some of the evidence to convict him, and I told him this group agreed. I told him in the letter that I could help him, something which I had not done in the fifteen years he had been on Death Row. I also told him that I needed some *security* so that I could feel safe. That's what he thought I was here for, *security*.

I had always told him that I wouldn't help him because of the publicity that it might bring, but that wasn't true. I didn't want him out. Like so many of *his* cons before, I was in this room for the complete opposite reason that he was so excited about. I was here to see that he never had a chance to get out, period. There was little chance of this anyway but he was optimistic about his appeals. This visit was about security alright, but not the kind he was thinking.

The beginning was the hardest part. It felt good to see him. He smiled, laughed and was as charming as ever. It made me long for the father I always thought he was, and for a brief moment I felt truly sorry for him. I was still incapable of putting both the killer and my father together in the same thought, I simply couldn't do it. I really wanted him to be that guy I loved and idolized, but the truth is that man never existed. This is the paradox that I lived with.

When we greeted each other, I had to feel those emotions of love to let him see them, because that is what he expected. I made it real for him and me, because as always, he was reading my emotions. That's what sociopaths do, and they are very good at it. Then I had to shake that off and get to business. I had prepared for this and now I was in it, alone with my father in a private room on Death Row with an audience, a wire and a recorder under my chair.

We talked for a while and exchanged pleasantries. We began to discuss the letter that I had sent, telling him what I wanted. This was the beginning of a dance of control and positioning. This was his game, so I let him run the show and played stupid, just as he had taught me. This always worked for him. Let the other person think he's got you by the balls because you're a dumb old fart, then turn the tables and pounce when he is blinded with greed and self-confidence. Give him more than enough rope to hang himself, and then yank on it with lightening speed and he'll never know what hit him. Little did I know that some of good old Dad's lessons would give me an advantage in facing evil itself.

Once we got into the conversation, I told him that I needed to have information that would make me feel safe before helping him get out. His entire demeanor changed. He sat back, considered what I had said, and smiled. He looked right at me with his cold eyes and said, "I get it . . . blackmail." Odd as it sounds, he seemed extremely proud of me for doing this. It appeared as if I was now playing his game. He was suddenly very engaged, and this was fun for him.

I started the conversation about murder by reminding him about the two black guys. I said, "Dad, you told me a story about two black guys seventeen years ago and I never said a word to you or anybody else about this since that night. Do you remember that conversation?"

He immediately looked directly into my eyes and said, "Yes, I appreciate the shit out of that!"

We spent about two hours together and he repeated everything I told the homicide detectives, basically word for word. He then described how he set up these two murders months earlier from the Atlanta Penitentiary.

He told the story with almost the same enthusiasm as when he first described it to me all those years ago. He was still particularly proud of how he was able to kill the second guy after he thought he had gotten away. Patiently waiting for him to return to the spot where he shot and killed his brother was his *favorite* part of the story. He liked describing how he waited and calmly pulled the trigger of his 12-gauge shotgun as his victim stood above his brother's mortally wounded body.

Looking back, it is amazing to me that I was able to hear that story again from him and stay completely focused on the task at hand. This was a terrifying moment in my life that I was revisiting and it wasn't being done in the comfort of a therapist's office. This was in the presence of evil on Death Row, with cold case detectives listening in from another room. The comfort that I felt was not coming from the outside, I assure you. It was kind of a numb, lifeless feeling. I was just going through the motions. This was a role with which I was very comfortable because this is the way it had always been with my father. Because he was familiar with it, too, it didn't seem unusual to him. I didn't know it at the time, but I simply slipped back into that role that hid *my* true character from him. There was some faith involved with this, but it wasn't the same peace that I have come to know today. It was different, yet still familiar to me.

He then went on to talk about the woman that he had murdered. This is the crime that placed him on Death Row, a conviction he was still denying to others and a case that was under appeal. There was some evidence presented in the case that he was disputing. He was mad as hell about it and said he had proof that they were fabricating evidence. His proof? He leaned across the table and said softly, "I was there! I know. I dragged her body fifty feet into the woods and the hair they said they found on her body was not possible!" Again, he said, "I was there! I dragged her. Do you understand what I'm saying to you? They lied!"

My approach to getting my father to talk had opened the door for him to tell me even more about this murder, and he liked that. Once again I had become his trusted confidante. Watching a sociopath justify murder, while questioning the integrity and loyalty of others, is a bizarre experience that is difficult to describe. There is absolutely no logic in this insane world, and it is impossible to rationalize anything you see or hear. Sociopaths live in chaos without boundaries, but hold everyone else accountable. In fact, if you break the same rules that they dismiss, their response is typically intense rage.

When talking about the killings, he lost himself in them. This was the only time that he wasn't concerned with me because he was so self-absorbed by it all. It felt good to him, as if he were reliving some great accomplishment. He was proud of it, except for getting caught of course, which he referred to as "stupid mistakes, sloppy". It was as if someone were telling you about having a child or some romantic getaway with a passionate lover, it was that deep. As he was describing the murders, he was experiencing the emotion of it, and I could see it again. After catching himself, he would calm down and mention that this was all bad, that he had changed. He said he was insane because of what *they* did to him, but he wouldn't ever do that again. He had learned his lesson, and when he got out, he was going to live in a trailer in the woods and quietly enjoy the rest of his life.

In the end, he would not confess to the final, unsolved murder that I was hoping he would talk about. This was the first murder that my father told me about in May of 1987, but he was much more discrete at the time. He used words such as, "he won't be around" or "he'll disappear" to describe what he was going to do to his lifelong friend and associate Bob Regan. Apparently giving me the details of killing *his friend* and telling me the location of the body was not something he thought I could handle. For now, I had to leave this one alone. I had what I came for.

When we finished he was sorry to see me go. He said this was the best visit he had had in fifteen years and he was excited that I was going to help him get out. After all, according to him, he had already served fifteen years, and if he had pleaded guilty he'd be getting out anyway. "They owe me," he said.

I hugged him and said goodbye, knowing that this was the

last time I would ever hug my father again. After this, getting too close to him was going to become life threatening. I enjoyed the feeling and let him go. As crazy as it sounds, *I love you, Dad*, is all that I was thinking. *I'm going to miss you*, or at least that image of you that I always held in my mind. An image that concealed a deadly killer.

Once back to the other room with detectives I felt relieved and extremely at ease. There was a guard there who knew my dad. I told him this was going to be hard on my dad and that I loved my father. I said I was just doing what I had to do. He smiled, looked me in the eye and said I admire what you did here today. I asked him to look after my dad and left.

I left Death Row for the last time, knowing I had done the right thing. I still had some mixed emotions, though. Even after seeing my father excited to talk about murders that he committed, I still felt sorry for him. I also knew what was coming his way. He was about to be visited by something he was very familiar with delivering to other people: Hell.

On the way home I stopped to have lunch with the very detectives who were about to bring that hell upon my father. I felt safe and comfortable, even though I had just gone through a very personal matter by ending a relationship with the only father I had ever known. As sick as it was, it was still a relationship of forty-five years, one that was the very foundation for all of my childhood memories.

It was at lunch with homicide detectives Allen Lee and Duwana Pelton of the Orange County Sheriff's Office that I realized how much I appreciated the work that these people do, especially these two. They became my friends that day. They were there to solve a case, but they also showed a great deal of compassion and understanding for what I had gone through. Detectives get dirty when they are protecting us, living in another world that we only visit from time to time. I have seen more and stayed longer than most, but like the rest of society, I get to leave the ugliness behind now. They live in it to protect us from it, and I am grateful for that, as we all should be.

On the rest of the drive home I continued to feel a great deal of pain about how my father was going to feel when he found out that, according to the code of his tortured world, I betrayed him. I was his favorite son, and now I was about to become his worst enemy. This is what separates me from him today. I thank God that I have these emotions and that I can feel compassion for others, even when some people don't think they deserve it.

This visit would lead to my father threatening to kill my family and telling me that he thinks about killing me twenty-four/seven, every moment of everyday. It is a threat that he cannot carry out from Death Row, and it absolutely tortures him that he cannot get to me. This is now his hell, one with which I am very familiar. Hell is where he took his family; we just didn't know what to call it.

Chapter 12

A Rising Death Toll—A Family Infected

I had suicidal thoughts as far back as I can remember. As a little kid, alone in my room at night, I would fantasize about how my dad and stepmother would feel if I died. I would try to hold my breath as long as I could, fighting the urge to breath with everything I had. It wasn't a trick like some kids do to get their parents attention; I was alone in my room at night when I tried this, hoping beyond hope that it would work. I wanted it to work.

Part of the motivation was so that my father and step-mother would realize just how much they missed me. I needed to show them that they loved me, and I figured that losing me would be the only way to make them see it. Still, this wasn't the only attraction to death for me. I simply didn't want to feel anymore.

This is how it was for us kids. This was our normal. As a kid you just don't know any better . . . intellectually, that is. But deep down within, there is something that tells us that things aren't right. As small children, we find this feeling of un-easiness very confusing because we have no perspective for it. Friends, family and outsiders all seem to act as if everything is okay, and we naturally assume that there must be something wrong with us.

I am really struggling to find the words to describe this feeling. It was like trying to deny that I knew my own father would stop loving me if I did something wrong and I might never get him back. I had a deep inner fear that my relationship with my father was always temporary, but this particular fear represented the truth: that's exactly what happened with my older brother.

According to my father, my brother consistently let him down. It was either his grades in school or always getting in trouble. My father talked to me about what a *loser* my brother was all the time. Without realizing it, I understood that not doing what my father wanted would cause him not to love me, so of course I did what he said. I was the good kid and now I know why. It was because my brother went before me. He didn't know any better. He was born in the middle of a mine field without instructions or a guide to help him, wandering aimlessly and stepping on mine after mine until he was ripped to pieces inside and out.

I think my dad enjoyed the pain that he delivered as punishment for childlike mistakes, because he could do it without compassion or remorse. It confirmed his power over others.

My older brother was his first child. He beat him, threw him out of the house and "disowned" him on more than one occasion. He told him that he was going to leave him a dollar in his will because he was a disgrace. He talked about my brother as if he belonged to someone else's family, always telling me what a screw up he was. He used to say that my brother "could fuck up a one car funeral." This is how I learned about the love of a father, from watching his treatment of my big brother. The lesson for me was that love comes with terms. Do what they ask, or lose it.

It's ironic that my father said these things about my brother and then proceeded to use him in his land fraud schemes. He used him as a "go for" and gave him drugs so that he could handle the pressure of the con. My brother helped my father sneak deeds and titles in and out of courthouses and posed as a landlord representative for property that my father would show to potential buyers. He once called an old woman on the phone screaming threats and obscenities at her until she stopped answering the phone, just in case someone tried to call her during a closing. The closing was for property that belonged to her, but of course, she didn't know her property was about to be sold. It was my brother's job to keep it that way.

One of the stories that demonstrates most clearly how my father treated my brother happened after the FBI came looking for my father about these land deals. Knowing that he was in trouble, my dad decided to start the marijuana farm. He bought a chicken farm on a hill and buried a semi tractor trailer in the ground to grow pot with hydroponics. He put my brother in charge. He considered my brother expendable, and that is why he continued to use him in risky situations. My father was also desperate at this point because he was facing possible prison time for his white-collar crimes.

My dad told me that my brother was messing things up. He said he couldn't trust him any more and needed to remove him from the situation, but he had a plan to get rid of him. To remove my brother from the situation, good old Dad hired a private investigator to act as an undercover police officer. He had my brother and me come to his office, and when this guy approached, he sent us into a back room where we could overhear the conversation. The fake cop said he had a warrant for my brother's arrest in the land deals, and was he very convincing about his desire to find him. Of course, Dad had no idea where he was and pretended to protect my brother, finally convincing this so-called cop to leave.

I have never seen my brother so scared. He was terrified. My father gave him some money and took him to the airport so that he could go to Miami and stay with our mom. I remember my brother calling from the airport, paranoid that the cops were looking for him everywhere. This created a whole new set of problems, because my brother was now afraid to go anywhere, especially my mom's house. He finally went, after some serious coaxing, but his stress level had been elevated and he was going to be living with this new fear for a while. Of course, the police were not looking for him and he was never questioned about his role in Dad's land swindles. I watched as my father celebrated his brilliant scheme. It made me sick to be a part of this.

My brother has dealt with alcohol and drug addiction his whole life and is currently serving twenty years for a DUI (his third) with serious bodily injury in Florida. He used heroin, methadone, oxycontin and basically anything that would help him escape from the pain.

I do not believe that there is such a thing as a *hopeless human condition.* I used to, but not anymore. I've seen too many miracles not to know they do happen, and my brother is in the midst of one. His recovery is not up to me, but the bottom line is that he was another casualty of my father's condition. He was definitely infected, but now his condition seems to be getting the treatment it needs. He is back in recovery and now helping others in prison. He is finally getting free.

As for my older sister, my dad despised women so much that she never had a chance. She was simply less worthy of his attention, almost a throwaway. My sister craved his love, as all little girls do, and he could not have cared less. She so wanted to be daddy's little girl. She did the right things and stayed out of trouble, but he still told me how worthless she was. She had no chance with him, absolutely none. This was family casualty number two.

My sister developed all kinds of mental and physical illnesses. She had every major mental illness that you can imagine, switching from one diagnosis to the other without questioning or recognizing that this was a problem. She was institutionalized for a brief period, blamed doctors for misdiagnosing her, and continued to self-diagnose her problems.

Just before she died in 2006, she told me that she had cat worms in her eyes. She said the doctor told her that she was crazy, and she was angry that no one believed her. I made fun of her at the time. It was just my crazy sister. Nobody took her seriously any more. She died a few weeks later, sitting in her lounge chair in an apartment the size of my closet. It was a mixture of drugs that finally just stopped her body, but no one called it an overdose. It was determined that she died of "natural causes" at the age of forty-seven. Right, that makes sense. No, this was another family casualty, a slow death that started almost from the day she was born.

While researching about sociopaths, I found an interesting connection to a disorder called Somatization Disorder. It is a possible outcome for a female child of a sociopath, and it described all of my sister's symptoms *including* the sensation of worms in her head. My sister wasn't only insane; she was infected with a family disease.

When my brother and I cleaned out her apartment I was surprised to see two old pictures above her very small bed. They were of my mom and dad from their twenties, almost like a shrine. One was a picture of my dad as an Air Force pilot and the other of my mom as the University of Miami Ibis Queen. Two beautiful pictures, but complete distortions of the truth.

It was absurd that a picture of the man who did this to her would be on her wall like some kind of honor. She died trying to recapture something that never existed. She spent her whole life chasing a dream that ironically, condemned her to living in a nightmare. My sister did not have a good life, and that's the truth of the matter.

Like my sister, as the child of a sociopath, I was also able to create my own image of my dad, one that left out the bad stuff. I don't know how I was able to do that, just that I did. It must be human nature I guess, or maybe has something to do with survival. Removing that veil is impossible for some, because what's behind it is so terrifying that we can't bear even to think about it. This is why my sister went to such extremes to reinforce that image of Dad.

As for my mom, she died at the age of fifty-four, twenty years before my sister. Lung cancer is what got her, but that wasn't all of it. She was another casualty. The coroner didn't include, "Life destroyed by a sociopath, the father of her children," on a death certificate. She lived a painful existence too.

My father destroyed my mother in a divorce, and she was an alcoholic. She never fully recovered from the divorce and died a slow painful death as she watched us kids idolize our dad, the very man that destroyed her. I am convinced that she knew how bad he was, and that killed her . . . literally. She had very little chance as well.

I was too young to remember, maybe three or four when my parents divorced, but I was told about how my father destroyed her in court to get custody of us kids. My mother left some writings behind. She wanted to write a book one day as well, and her notes were very revealing. She wrote about how my father tried to have her raped by a mutual friend so that he could use it against her in court.

I loved my mom and she had a great heart, but she was not a very good mother. It pains me to say that, but I love her just the same. Like my sister, it is hardest for me to pull the veil back on my mother. I don't want to see her as flawed human being. I prefer to think of her as a beautiful lady, but I had some very traumatic experiences with her alcoholism as a child. I needed a mother and she was not very dependable. In truth, there were times when my mother became a liability and put me in life-threatening situations. I'll leave it at that.

One of the most emotional moments that I ever had was visiting her gravesite in 2004 after all these memories came back to me. I wrote her a letter and told her how I felt. All of it, good and bad. I got on my knees in front of her gravesite and read it to her, forgave her, and then I asked her for forgiveness.

I told her that I was sorry for choosing my father over her, that I didn't know any better and that I forgave her for not being a better mom. That was the hardest thing for me to say to her, but I needed to tell her the truth. I needed to tell myself the truth. I burned the letter and sat before her for a long period of time just crying and telling her that I loved her anyway. I knew she did the best that she could with what she was given. I told her that and thanked her for what she did for us.

My mom did love us. It was real love, and I thank her and God for that. I think the only reason I know what love is today is because she taught me. For that, I am forever grateful. I do have many great memories of her. The truth of the matter is that I wasn't a very good son either. We were all screwed up. This is a family disease, and we all had it, but her love is the gift that got through to me. I will always remember her for that.

The pain was not restricted to my immediate family, but also had an effect on my half-brother and half-sister, uncles, aunts, cousins . . . everybody. I suppose each has their own difficulties to face, on their own time. Some don't talk to me to this day and others are very close. I am not to judge, only to love them all.

As I looked more closely at my family and my past, I began to understand why I did the things that I did as a child and as an adult. The Truth about me was beginning to be revealed. It had always been there, but I just wasn't willing to look for it.

I was too scared.

Chapter 13

Fear Mongers—Tools of Engagement

To conquer fear is the beginning of wisdom.
—Bertrand Russell

When I was a kid my older brother used to tell me scary stories right before we went to bed. We shared a room together, and his purpose was to scare the hell out of me so that I wouldn't be able to sleep. It is amazing how that affected me, but even more amazing was what it did to him. He would wake up in the middle of the night, sit straight up in his bed, and scream at the top of his lungs. He was having horrible nightmares. His terrifying screams were always worse for me than the stories themselves, because his fear seemed so real. I know it was real to him, because I could see the terror in his face.

I may not be qualified to analyze my brother's behavior, but it seemed to me that there were a couple of things going on here. One was the simple fact that we were being raised by a sociopath and some of this was simply a response to a deep-rooted fear and uneasiness that we kids lived with.

My brother was giving me the only thing that he knew to give away, fear. This is what my father was giving him, and he instinctively was passing on to others what had been given so freely to him. Another way to put it is to say that he was trying to give away something that he had too much of, but didn't want.

Without realizing it, we are constantly giving away what-ever it is that we have at that particular moment. If we are angry, that is typically what we will offer the person that is in front of us. When we are happy and full of love, that is what we will most likely attempt to pass on to others. This is a fairly simplistic way of demonstrating that age-old spiritual truth that *to give is the same as to receive.* Just as this holds true so does the wisdom that whatever you give, you will receive in return. My brother wasn't just telling *me* scary stories, he was telling them to *himself*, and the result was intense fear.

You are what you pay attention to, and my brother was obsessed with scaring people. As a result, that's what he got . . . scared. The same holds true for me. If I tell myself scary stories, I am going to get scared. This lesson helps me to begin to understand the very nature of fear and how it works. It is evil and understanding how it operates has been the most difficult, challenging, exhilarating and freeing journey that I have ever taken.

Fear is found throughout scripture and is most often referred to as evil. Its offspring are worry, anxiety, anger and rage. In extreme cases, such as my father, fear can lead to un-warranted pride, a profound sense of entitlement and vengeful resentments that result in a complete commitment to ego. The sociopath's response to fear is an extraordinary commitment to self. This self is not grounded within, but an illusion created entirely in the mind. This disconnects the sociopath from their inner self, virtually burning the spiritual bridge that connects the rest of us to a higher power. This leaves no room for a conscience, resulting in a need to control others for their life's experiences and energy, reducing them to creatures that are more like spiritual vampires. Sociopaths live life off of the re-sources of others. This is their source of power and its fuel is fear.

My observations are not grounded in medical research but in firsthand experience, and this is what it looks like to me. In-tense fear can lead us in one of two directions: towards faith in search of a higher power, or away towards self-reliance. Most people seem to live somewhere in the middle of this spectrum.

Many move more deeply towards faith and enlightenment, but a small minority chooses to move *completely* away from faith in a higher power. My suspicion is that fear is the basis for this commitment. Research estimates that more than four percent of society is sociopathic. Why sociopaths choose fear over faith seems to have a lot to do with genetics and the environment that they are raised, but regardless, this is still a spiritual disease.

It seems possible that in some cases a child might find himself so filled with fear and frightened with no tools to deal with it that the only choice becomes a commitment to self. This self convinces the child that in order to remove this fear they must *control* the environment around them. In order to do this, one must be able to disregard the feelings of others. This complete disregard for others feelings becomes possible only when one determines that the personal gain is worth it— resulting in an utter loss of conscience.

One of my favorite quotes is, *Courage is not the absence of fear, but rather the judgment that something else is more important than fear.* In most cases, that "something else" is peace and happiness and they lead to faith. As an alternative choice, is it possible to choose your self/ego as the way to alleviate these fears. If you are convinced you can control everything around you, you will no longer have anything to fear.

I am absolutely certain that my father had fear. In fact his greatest fears were about a loss of control, which scared him. Controlling others was where he found his power and he had no other source. I believe that the sociopath lives in fear because self-reliance, even without the boundaries of society, will always fail us. They instinctively know this, as we all do. They remove all boundaries because they convince themselves that self-reliance with boundaries is weak and cannot possibly be enough to remove their fears.

As with a drug addiction, controlling others at all cost becomes the focal point of a sociopath's existence. My dad started out as a conman, but that too failed him and he was terrified. When he was sent to prison, I know for a fact it was fear that overwhelmed him. He spent three years, in his mind, fantasizing about exercising more control when he got out. He convinced himself that his failure was a lack of commitment to his guilt-free mind and he dreamed of killing people. He had this wonderful gift of being able to do things that others couldn't do and it failed him. This led to rage and an even deeper commitment to his inner desires of control.

While my father was in prison he planned to kill at least five people. His first victim, a lifetime associate and so-called friend, was killed within two months. He had dreamed of this murder and now he was back in control. Actually, more control than he had ever experienced. This new behavior was driven by fear turned to rage, now being expressed in reality as pleasure, and bringing him a false sense of peace. It was a total fraud of an emotion, but real to him.

The problem was that this "high" was extremely temporary, and the only way to keep fear at bay was to exercise more control over the world. As long as the sociopath is controlling others he feels safe, making murder the ultimate treatment for fear. Sociopaths believe that they are free from fear, but nothing could be further from the truth. They are only free when they are controlling and this takes an incredible amount of forceful effort and energy. That is why they always fail in the end. It is just not possible to sustain this way of life, and we are not created to be separate from our Creator. There is simply too much resistance and negative energy created by this way of living and it eventually catches up with the sociopath. He or She has no other power to rely upon and this eventually leads to annihilation.

Like my brother, my father was obsessed with fear. He delivered it to others for his own survival, but he wound up attracting it to himself. He now lives on Death Row where he has no control of others, and they all know his game. This is the ultimate punishment for the sociopath. He lives in an environment that takes away his only means of survival and control. I am convinced that my father lives in fear. He may fantasize about killing me or others, but that is an insufficient substitute for the real thing. He is truly torturing himself in his mind and his keeper is fear. He could run from it, but he could not hide. He acted on the scary stories that he was telling himself, and now living in one has become his reality. *A nightmare of a reality that he unknowingly created for himself.*

Just as my father did, my own ego uses fear to leverage its control over me. It creates unnecessary alarm within my mind, and the more intense the fear, the greater its power. My ego is the sociopath within, operating without conscience, held in check only by my existing connection to a higher power, the one abandoned by the true sociopath.

Today, I understand that the cause of almost all of my fears is based on self-reliance, which is simply a lack of faith. As I began to develop my faith I became a voracious reader, picking up almost every spiritual book that I could find. Most of them had a common message, and I started to recognize the truth in them. Some I discarded because they didn't resonate with my heart. There was something within me that was beginning to see the truth.

More than one book I read focused on the teachings of Jesus Christ. I prefer not to get into my own person beliefs because I think that can be a distraction. To my knowledge, I have no examples of people being excluded from the truth or a spiritual awakening because they didn't believe in something specific. All they needed was to take certain steps and develop a relationship with a God of their own understanding.

Anyway, at least two of these books simply stated that no matter what you believe, it is hard not to recognize Jesus as the most famous spiritual teacher in history. No other human being can be said to have had a greater impact on mankind than Jesus Christ. There is really no argument here, and some of these books looked at him primarily as a teacher and left the rest up to the reader. It is what he taught us that is so important. His teachings were found in virtually every other spiritual book worth its salt, whether they mentioned him directly or not.

When I began to learn about these spiritual teachings, the biggest question was: Is it true? They all speak of a life free from fear and worry, and that didn't sound possible to me, at least not at first, still something inside of me was connecting with this message. This led me to my next question . . . either he meant what he said, or he didn't. If he didn't, then everything that is built upon his teachings was built upon a lie. It was really that simple.

There is something that I learned on my own, which is: a lie cannot stand the test of time, period. The truth is the truth and will always be the truth. In addition, because I was finding the same exact teachings in other spiritual books, I decided to open my mind to the possibility that the promises Jesus made were true. This willingness to open my mind to the possibility that I might live in peace without fear opened a window into my soul. It gave me the courage I needed to begin to trust a power greater than myself for everything that I needed.

Again, courage is not the absence of fear, but rather the judgment that something else is more important than fear. For me, that something else was peace and happiness. I was raised to believe that faith was weakness. Now I believed for the first time that faith was the way of strength. The verdict of the ages is that all men of true faith have courage. For me, believing this is possible was the easy part; learning to live it is quite another story.

I always thought that faith was an intellectual decision to believe in something that you could not know and to live by the rules that go with that belief in hopes of being rewarded at the end of your life. This is how I understood faith and this concept seemed impossible. Now I was learning that by taking certain steps, and through the repetition of practicing certain principles in my life, that faith would come naturally. It was also something that I would not only come to know, but also feel and know intimately. I came to believe that the spiritual experience that I had was not an illusion, but a glimpse of heaven on earth. This state of grace had allowed me, for the first time, to experience life without the burden of fear, removing the main blocker between me and God.

It became very clear to me that fear *was* the problem. Nothing else so effectively robs the mind of all its power of acting and reasoning as fear. Now came the tricky part. First identifying it, then facing it, and finally taking the necessary steps to attempt to remove it from my life.

I was very fortunate to come in contact with spiritual teachers that were willing to show me the way. The primary lesson that they were sharing was the importance of presence, of being in the now. This was consistent with all the other books that I was reading, including the Bible. Almost all of my fear was coming from projecting future events, events that had not yet happened and didn't exist. The fear was from trying to work out these events in my mind to my satisfaction, which I came to learn was not possible.

Once I worked out a series of events in my mind, they would suddenly change, like a phantom, and I would start the process all over again. These projections were almost always concerned with my not getting something I wanted in the future or of losing something that I thought was important to me. The most amazing part that I learned was how I would actually take on the feelings of these bad events at the time that I was thinking about them, without them actually happening. I was beginning to see the futility in this, or more appropriately, the insanity of it. I was ruining the current moment by responding to thoughts of events in the future that were not real.

Then I was taught that all emotions are simply a response to thoughts. So the problem was in the thinking, since the events were not real. This was really beginning to make sense. Basically, I was telling myself scary stories and making myself believe them when there was absolutely no truth to them. If I can't predict what is going to happen five minutes from now, I am certainly not qualified to project about events that require millions, if not billions, of smaller events and people to line up just right to make it so.

Projecting about a meeting you might have with someone tomorrow will require an extraordinary number of events to line up for the meeting to happen exactly the way you imagine it. This would require you to determine in your mind what the other person might be thinking, feeling, and what they will say. Once I became aware of just how hard it was for me to understand my own thinking, it made me laugh at the insanity of trying to predict someone else's thoughts and attempting to determine what they *might* say so that I could work out the right response. Even more insane is not recognizing that trying to control a conversation prevents me from actually listening to what the other person is saying anyway. Listening, I have come to understand, is the most important gift that we have to offer another person.

Knowing this was only the first step, it didn't stop me from doing it, but at least I was armed now. Someone told me that my mind was a scary place to visit and that I shouldn't go there alone. Now it was time to enter armed, and my weapon was awareness.

One of the most common quoted passages in the Bible is probably one of the least trusted. Jesus said:

> "Therefore I tell you, do not worry about your life, what you will eat or drink; or about your body, what you will wear. Is not life more important than food, and the body more important than clothes? Look at the birds of the air; they do not sow or reap or store away in barns, and yet your heavenly Father feeds them. Are you not much more valuable than they? Who of you by worrying can add a single hour to his life?
>
> "And why do you worry about clothes? See how the lilies of the field grow. They do not labor or spin.

"But seek first his kingdom and his righteousness, and all these things will be given to you as well. Therefore do not worry about tomorrow, for tomorrow will worry about itself. Each day has enough trouble of its own."

—Matthew 6:25-34

The first time I read this it seemed like a foreign language, or at the very least, total nonsense. This made absolutely no sense to me. All I could see in this statement was a position of *give up*; it didn't look much like courage at all, at least not to me. This didn't make sense until I read other spiritual books that made similar statements a little more clearly, and then it really became clear when I started to study Jesus' teachings.

Once I read it a few times, I started to see the absolute simplicity of this teaching. Our *"heavenly Father"* supplies all living things with everything they need, why should we be any different? My initial response was, well if I don't take care of myself, I'll die. This is the result of a lack of trust in God. I had so little experience with this. I thought if I focused on God instead of my needs, I would somehow be caught in no man's land unable to function. The thought of relying on God for everything seemed like an impossible request that would result in the opposite outcome. This was because I had no repetition with this level of faith and still did not believe that God worked with me, through me. I had never tried it. My belief seemed to be that I would be putting my cares and worries into some powerless vacuum.

In practice, it is quite the opposite. Our thought life is placed upon a much higher plain when cleared of worry and fear. When we ask God for inspiration we often find that the right answers will come after we have practiced this for a while. What was once an occasional inspiration becomes a routine part of our thinking. We become much more efficient.

I get that we are much *"more valuable than they,"* but where the rest of it really started to make sense for me is in the phrase, *"Who of you by worrying can add a single hour to his life?"* This simple statement makes perfect sense, probably to almost everyone. Once I started to get part of this, it opened my mind to reevaluate the rest of it. This sentence sums up the first part and the message is *not to worry.* Jesus does not tell us to do nothing. In fact, everything he taught carried the message that faith without works is dead, but that is how it sounded to me and I know why. I believed that worry was required for action. I thought I needed to worry to be prompted to take action about certain things. This is not only a lie, it is wrong, and the results of this type of thinking can be catastrophic. That is why he consistently warned us about this, calling it sin. Sin, as I understand it now, simply means *missed the mark.*

The part about the *lilies* I used to find amusing. This sounded like a worthless existence, but quite the contrary. The reference is that the lily grows with life, does not resist it. This simple statement contains magic for me. If you want to experience life to the fullest, the best way to do it is make peace with it, accept *what is* and be present. When I do this, miracles happen.

The final part is my favorite, because it tells me exactly what I am supposed to do.

> "But seek first his kingdom and his righteousness, and all these things will be given to you as well. Therefore do not worry about tomorrow, for tomorrow will worry about itself. Each day has enough trouble of its own."
>
> —Matthew 6:33-34

Simple, but it is extremely difficult to do. The first and most difficult step is to believe it's possible to live this way. The rest is all about getting there. Like many others before me, once I became willing, as difficult as it seemed at times, I began to recognize a power greater than myself helping me with this process, especially during times of great doubt and inner conflict. Unlike my biological father, this father not only wants the best for me, he is also my helper. When I trust him, it works. When I don't, I go it alone. I now have a choice. I can choose to trust and stop worrying about the future, or . . . go it alone.

This always struck me as simply being a cop out. I don't know how else to put it. It just seemed like a lot to give up to me. I mean, come on, live like the lilies of the field and seek first the kingdom of God? This may sound like an excuse for those who can't handle life, but nothing could be further from the truth.

Actually, it's insanity *not* to do this. The truth is that arguing with what "already is" makes no sense whatsoever. Most people spend their entire lives obsessed with things that they cannot change. The result is pain, misery and suffering . . . and for what? Accepting *what is* is one of the simplest and most freeing lessons that I have ever learned. It seems to me that many people confuse this with accepting failure in the future, but that is not what this says. This is about accepting that which already exists, things that we cannot change. Once I accept things that I cannot change I am no longer distracted by the past and can focus on the present. I am only then able to be happy and effective in handling what is in front of me at the time (*the trouble of each day*).

Seeking the Kingdom first also makes sense once you realize that the only real power in the universe is from God, and besides, it works. Courageous and faithful men have proven this time and time again throughout history.

This journey took me through some scary places that, at times, made me want to quit. The term, "gnashing of teeth" comes to mind when I think about it, but I wasn't *alone*. I began to learn that I could rely upon a higher power for shelter at times of incredible suffering. I was told that fear was simply vapor. It was simply a response to thought that existed only in my mind, but hearing these words wasn't enough to make it go away.

Trust takes practice, repetition and a commitment to a belief that God has all power. I wake up every morning in gratitude. My first thought as I wake is of God and thanks. I then follow that with a period of prayer and meditation. It is a daily ritual that seeks first the kingdom of peace before the distractions of the world have a chance to enter. It is a daily reprieve from fear, based on the maintenance of my spiritual condition and it works.

My ego wants to be my higher power, and I must deal with this on a daily basis. It has an awareness of its own that is intensely concerned with survival, and it will tell me anything it feels will preserve itself when it feels threatened. One of its most clever tricks is punishing me for what *it* has done to me while placing the blame squarely on God. *Do these characteristics sound familiar?*

The ego's primary weapon is fear and it delivers it by telling me scary stories that are not real. This pattern is very difficult to recognize when faced with extremely difficult circumstances that life sometimes brings, but this is where the greatest battles are fought and won. The ego has to be smashed, and this can be very scary. This is the bridge to spiritual freedom and is very often accomplished in times of great trial and tribulation. The Bible is full of stories that demonstrate this experience, as well as great wisdom on how to win these battles and how to claim the incredible promises that follow faithful endurance through this transformation.

As I wrote this, I was faced with some extremely challenging issues. My business had failed, and I had been struggling to overcome the fear associated with this experience, attempting to practice this while *I was in the fire*. When faced with not being able to support my family, failing to meet my obligations and the possibility of losing my home it seemed almost impossible to be spiritual, much less not to worry. My ego wants to tell me that when all this is settled, I'll be able to be spiritual, but this is another lie. Oftentimes these extremely challenging circumstances provide us the opportunity to make that leap of faith. In fact, we are experiencing them for this very reason.

I am not suggesting that God punishes us for this purpose, but I do believe that the circumstances resulting from our wrong thinking are used as lessons and opportunities for spiritual growth. Another phrase I love is *pain is the touchstone of spiritual growth.* Everything about my past confirms that this is true, *if* I allow it to be. The amazing part is that while it is happening my mind wants to tell me the opposite: that God will let me down this time and that believing will fail me. Therefore if the problem centers in the mind, then this is where I must focus my attention. Change my thinking and change my circumstances, or more appropriately . . .

"But seek first his kingdom and his righteousness, and all these things will be given to you as well."
—Matthew 6:33

My wrong thinking continued to project horrible outcomes to difficult situations in my life and tried to convince me that I was crazy for not worrying about it. It consistently projected outcomes of total loss of control if I stopped worrying, projecting catastrophe if I let go of this old familiar habit. Some of this was realized, not in spite of my worrying, but because of it. Like my father, I am creating my own reality. This can be both frightening and liberating at the same time. We are not victims, but participants in life.

Fortunately, as I mentioned before, I had some wonderful people around me who continued to teach me. One of the simplest lessons was to "doubt the doubt." My friend said that I had no business projecting, but if thoughts of scary future events came into my mind, I should question them . . . "doubt the doubt," he said. He explained to me how when he went through a similar transformation he began to say to himself, "What the hell do you know, you can't predict the future". This simple message made sense to me and I began to practice it. I was told to focus completely on the Now and leave the rest up to God. It was a scary leap, but when I did it, miracles happened. Circumstances suddenly lined up, and difficult situations were resolved.

As the risks I took in business began to catch up with me and the economy took a sudden turn for the worse, I was left in an unthinkable situation. I could not cover my obligations to my customers and was propelled into a feeling of hopelessness once again. Only this time I was armed with the tools of engagement and began to apply them to this particular situation. Could I change my circumstances by changing my thinking first?

The day that this problem was removed from me, I was not thinking about it. I was totally focused on the present as I was being taught. I dismissed all fear and projection the moment it entered my mind. I was into action, not thinking. Interestingly enough, I was presented with a dilemma that day. A desperate friend in need called and asked for my help. My initial response was "not now" because I had too many "problems" of my own to deal with, then I remembered what I was taught, and that was; *it is better to give than to receive and that if I took care of God's business, He would take care of mine.* I therefore agreed to meet and help this friend.

While meeting with her, the thought *from my ego* of just how insane this was entered my mind. I dismissed the though reminding myself not to project and to be present, allowing a higher power to work through me to help this person. Within two hours of this meeting, this particular problem was resolved by a scenario that I never projected as a possible solution. It was an immediate and complete solution and I recognized what it was the instant it happened.

It works if you work it and you can only experience this by doing it. I will overcome if I seek first the kingdom of God, and then all these other things will be added to me as promised. But I have to do the work. If it were self-reliance that had failed me, it will be faith in an infinite God not my finite self that is going to save me.

Here's the most interesting part for me. It was great that almost-impossible circumstances were suddenly resolved, but the real rush came from knowing that God had helped me. This, for me, is the treasure. Forget the circumstances, experiencing this is almost indescribable. I had a rush of goose bumps and a connectedness that brought tears to my eyes. The feeling was one of overwhelming gratitude, love and laughter. Yes, laughter. After one of these experiences I laughed with God at the humor of it all. I was scared of nothing and my real father had my back the whole time. There was joy in this experience, including a sense that "my father" enjoyed this experience just as much, if not more than I did.

As a father myself, I can understand this. It's like teaching my kid to ride a bike. In the beginning, I was right there with her, but as her trust began to build I gave her more room, more responsibility. She fell a couple of times, but I allowed that because it was part of learning. It may have hurt when she fell, but I was always there when she needed me. She was always safe. I gave her just enough room to learn. The more she trusted me, the better she did. When she got scared, she fell. This was teaching her that faith and trust work, but fear doesn't. In the end, once she trusted me, she rode down the street as happy as she could be. As a father, this simple lesson was extremely gratifying, and I imagine my heavenly father feels the same way.

I had always heard people talk about having a personal relationship with God, and I could not understand that. I believed it was in their imagination, a story they told themselves to feel secure. Now I know what it means, because when a relationship with God happens it is personal and it is magnificent—like nothing I've ever known before. I certainly scraped my knees a few times, but finally with the help of others, I was beginning to see that these scrapes were the result of fear and my wrong thinking, not the other way around. Worrying is like praying for something bad to happen and that is exactly what I had been doing. I had been blaming God for what my ego was doing to me.

As I've mentioned before, I have read many spiritual books, and while I believe that everyone has a different path to a spiritual awakening, they *all* seem to have one thing in common. Once you start down this path, if you continue to seek it and ask for help, you will receive it. That's the truth as I understand it.

> "Ask and it will be given to you; seek and you will find; knock and the door will be opened to you.
> "For everyone who asks receives; he who seeks finds; and to him who knocks, the door will be opened."
>
> —Matthew 7:7-8

God always answers, but it's up to us to knock. This door is the gateway to peace, but some of us have to go through hell and scrape our knees a few times before we get it. How much suffering has a lot to do with each individual's ability to stop listening to the scary stories we tell ourselves.

It's difficult to make sense of all this, and I am not equipped to help anyone else try to explain their own difficulties and tragedies. I can only share my experience. What I do know is this. When I look deep within myself, I can see where nearly every trouble in my life has originated. It is not a blame game, but something called spiritual growth and the rewards are indescribable.

Why things are like this, I have no idea, but for me it is incredibly liberating. What I think, what I do has an impact on what is manifested in my life. Everything I do or even think has an effect on my world. *What I see I have asked for.* This in itself can be a scary proposition, but there is one who has all power, and he wants to help us overcome this fear.

That was good to know, because I was headed back to hell for another look.

Chapter 14

Finding My Way Out of Hell

Hell is not something experienced on the outside. As much as I'd like to think that my experience with my father is to blame for everything bad that happened to me, it is just not true. Hell is created on the inside, by our own doing. It's what we do with the experiences that determine where we live. It is a choice between heaven and hell . . . literally.

Real freedom from fear comes through release from the past. At least, that has been my experience. This release occurs when we realize that the past has no power over us. In order to accomplish this, we must first get down to the causes and conditions that altered our God-given instincts in the first place.

If peace is the destination that I am seeking, and I am, then there must be a starting point. Anytime that I seek directions to a particular destination, the first question that I am asked is always the same: "Where are you coming from?" I can't get there from here if I don't know where *here* is.

Recovery is all about specific steps. First we admit that we are powerless over whatever it is that has brought us to our knees. Next, we recognize that we were unable to restore ourselves to sanity, so some power greater than ourselves would be needed to survive. Consequently, we make a decision to turn our will and our lives over to the care of God *as we understand him.* Then we commence to search out things in ourselves which had brought us to physical, moral, and spiritual bankruptcy. This is one of the most important steps.

In the twelve steps this process begins with the fourth step when we agree to take a "fearless and moral inventory of ourselves."

I understood this to mean that I needed to find exactly when and where these God-given instincts were altered. Simplified, when did I decide that I was separate from life and lose all trust in a higher power of any kind, at which point I was led to depend upon self-reliance for my very survival?

I was told that many people drink to cover up this loss of trust, and this symptom appears well after this change occurs. Since, I began drinking excessively at a very early age (as early as twelve years old) the loss must have been something that happened long before that.

Through recovery—and well after discovering the memories of the murders that my father told me about—I continued to take personal inventory of myself. It was extremely important that I go back through my past. I learned that nothing counted but thoroughness and honesty.

One technique I used was to sit quietly in mediation and begin to imagine that I was sitting in my living room about to enter the basement. I would say a prayer and invite God in, then leave all the sounds of the world behind as I opened the door to this basement. I imagined myself slowly walking down the steps to the basement, and there I began to survey the room. It was dimly lit, and there were imaginary boxes all over the floor. These boxes represented childhood memories and experiences, some I recognized and some I did not.

I would open a box and absorb the experience in it. I tried not to force this or create a memory, but let it come to me. Some of the memories were painful at first, but they brought a strange sense of comfort with them. It was painful, but comforting. That may sound odd, but I do not know how else to describe it.

Many involved my mother, and I moved through them until I found a box that struck me as being extremely im-portant. All were important, but some were already very familiar to me. I was looking for the ones that contained a high level of emotion but did not seem familiar. I was looking for the ones that I had buried here in the basement of my soul because they were too painful to think about.

I was taught by others that the most common experience that creates this change in us comes from a feeling of abandonment at a very early age. This can happen in what appears to be relatively normal families. In fact, often times, it is simply a misunderstanding of reality that our parents never even know occurred. It could be as simple as a parent accidentally forgetting to pick us up from somewhere. We don't understand why, and we create our own explanations. We might, for example, convince ourselves that we are not worthy of their love.

In some cases, however, it is extreme . . . and very real. In my case, I stumbled upon a particular experience that happened when I was probably four or five years old. It was a memory that was emotionally charged and brought me to tears. This was exactly what I was looking for in the basement. I opened the box, said another prayer asking for guidance, and took it all in.

As of yet, I have been unable to recover any memories of my mom and dad together. They divorced in 1964 when I was four years old. I do know that my mother was an alcoholic and that my brother witnessed her having sex with another man. Obviously, I was already being exposed to some serious trauma, probably from birth.

The earliest and most traumatic memory that I have been able to uncover thus far is when my stepmother entered the picture. At this early age I had not received the love I so desperately needed from my father or my mother. I felt that my mother had abandoned me, both as a drunk and then literally as a result of the divorce. Under those circumstances I met my future stepmother.

Like my father, she was incredibly charming. I am sure that she was trying to win over us kids, which would be why she gave us a lot of attention. She was thirteen years younger than my father, very attractive and incredibly sweet. Or so I thought. Like my father, she was hiding her true nature from us, and I was about to be betrayed again.

I was desperate for love, and she seemed to be the answer. My dad didn't have it to give, and my mom seemed to care more about getting drunk. My stepmother was a welcome addition to the family and I fell in love with her. At least that's what I called it.

Before they got married and she moved into the house, I would yearn for her attention when she was not around. My most vivid memory is of her smell. She wore a perfume that was wonderfully sweet, and the smell of it comforted me. I don't know if I did this more than once, but I do remember curling up with her soft white robe because of the smell on it and finding great peace and comfort in it. I can totally relate to a family dog that wants to curl up on his master's bed and pillows because of the comfort that the smell brings while the master is away.

The truth about my new safe harbor was not revealed until after they married, but when it came, it was definitive and final. There may have been some signs leading up to this, but I don't remember them. The event that I do remember, however, was when I decided that I was completely and forever alone in an alien world.

I was walking through the kitchen to the dining room to join my *new* family for dinner and dropped my milk glass. My stepmother screamed in anger at me for this incredible act of stupidity, and it startled me so much that I dropped my plate of spaghetti.

As she unleashed uncontrollable rage upon me, I began to cry, and this only made it worse. Now, she said, I was being a pitiful, weak little kid, and she was obviously disappointed in me. I don't remember what I said, but when I spoke, I addressed her as "Mom". She chose that moment to correct me and clearly defined our relationship forever.

She screamed, "I am not your mother, never was, never will be! From now on CALL ME JANE!" At that very moment I *decided* that I was alone, completely alone. I had suspected that all along, but this was the final confirmation that I was not loveable. She was my last hope for the love of a parent, and that door was closed, slammed shut without any reservation whatsoever. *This is where the separation occurred.* Now that this door was closed, she was free to open another, the one that would reveal her true character. Those characteristics were frighteningly familiar.

This is one example of many experiences that I have found through deep self-exploration. I have been taught to continue to look deep within myself whenever I feel blocked or disturbed—particularly if my response to a certain event or situation is not proportionate to what the situation calls for. These become opportunities for healing and spiritual growth. It is through this type of work that I was able to clear away the wreckage of the past and open the door to forgiveness and peace.

One of my daily rituals as suggested in the steps is to sit quietly before going to bed and to review my day. The suggestion is to look carefully at all my relationships from the day and to ask myself if there were opportunities to be more kind and loving to others. This is not to be critical of myself, but only to look at where I might do better the next time. If I do find something that doesn't feel right, I can promptly make amends and correct it.

It is also a time to look at the positive side of the balance sheet for things done well. My days now are filled with many kind acts of compassion and accomplishment. Sometimes I might recall something particularly disturbing or some emotions that are obviously disproportionate to what the situation called for, but when this happens, I go searching for the cause. If I am to correct the situation I will need to know exactly when and where this alteration of my instincts occurred. As I do this, I am correcting my misperception of past events.

Recently, I found myself having an issue with reading in a group environment. I was feeling an incredible amount of anxiety, and I couldn't seem to catch my breath. It was very strange because I do a great deal of public speaking and have very little fear of speaking in front of an audience. I understand that most people feel some anxiety when they do this, but this was different. It was as if I was terror-stricken. It was an obvious overreaction to the circumstances, and I started to seek the cause of it. I went back to the basement in my morning meditation.

As I was looking through my childhood past, I found an event at school where I was absolutely terrified while reading in front of a group. This memory was from the sixth grade, but I realized that this event was just an expression of an already underlying problem. I had to go back further. As it so often does when I do this type of deep work, the memory just came to me suddenly. It was not forced.

In this childhood memory, my stepmother was punishing me for not being able to read to her from a book without crying. I was struggling with my reading homework, and she was frustrated, standing in front of me across the kitchen table. She started screaming at me and made me try again to get it right. Each time it became more and more difficult as the pressure mounted. I would read a few words and then begin to hyperventilate, paralyzed with fear. I began to cry uncontrollably, and my tears only increased her anger. She then grabbed me by the neck of my shirt and run me down the hallway, whipping me across the legs with a flyswatter with every step.

This was repeated over and over again until I simply couldn't bear it any more. The only way to end this terror was to read without crying and I just couldn't do it. I was kept back in second grade. I believed it was because I wasn't smart enough, and I hated myself for it. In fact, without realizing it, I was learning how to treat myself for these miserable failures from my stepmother.

This process of opening myself to the past, teaches me to understand the reasons for some of the things I do and feel today. Everything in my life is experienced through this filter— a filter that is often very inaccurate, resulting in a distorted view of the world. The problem when I was a child was not the reading itself, but the altered belief that there was tremendous risk associated with the task of getting this right, a risk that really didn't exist.

If you saw a big stick or a black rubber hose on the side of the road, you might think that it's a snake. Out of the corner of your eye, it might look like a snake, and that may result in an initial response that is disproportionate to what the situation calls for. At this point you can choose to respond to the fear and flee, or you can summon the courage to take a closer look and examine the evidence. Someone who has been bitten by a snake as a young child may have a much more difficult time overcoming the initial fear and would be much more afraid to look more closely at it. We often misunderstand current events when viewed through this filter of past experiences, many of them formed when we were little children and didn't know any better.

If we take the time to examine this behavior thoroughly and honestly in the presence of our creator and with another human being, as suggested, we are likely to find that we are simply responding to imaginary threats that turn out to be harmless shadows. This examination allows us to understand better the past and to place it in its proper perspective, freeing us from this unnecessary fear and anxiety of the unknown. Once these experiences are exposed to the light, we find that they no longer have any power over us. In fact, the only power that they ever held over us was that which we unknowingly gave them.

Something else miraculous began to happen to me as I continued with this process. I was taught to look not only at the wrongs that others had done, but also to look resolutely for my own mistakes. The inventory is ours, not the other persons.

Once I admitted my wrongs honestly and became willing to set matters straight, an overwhelming sense of compassion and forgiveness for the other person began to fill my heart.

For the first time I began to see people who hurt me as fellow sufferers, people with whom I could identify. For example, I came to understand that my stepmother did the best that she could with what she had. She did the best that she could, given the tools that she had to deal with life. There is no telling what caused her to be the way she was, but she must have been in a great deal of pain to want to hurt children. She was only trying to give away what she didn't want.

The same holds true for my father. If he, as a sociopath, is incapable of love how could I continue to hold him accountable for something that he couldn't give me? How much pain must he have been in, if he believed that killing people would make him feel better? If you place no value on another man's life, what does that say about your own? Offering forgiveness does not make it okay to do harmful things, but it does add some perspective and compassion to what we are seeing in the people that may have harmed us in our lives.

This forgiveness is the pathway to healing, but the real purpose of this house-cleaning exercise is to remove those spiritual blockers that have been preventing us from trusting God with all of our difficulties. I think everyone can relate an experience in their lives where at some point they asked in desperation for God's help and miraculously received it. Very few, however, believe God plays a role in everything that we do.

I understand this dilemma because I have been there, and I still go there from time to time. It is very difficult to believe that God is in us, participating in our lives and willing to help us with any situation in which we are able to invite him. All of our difficulties can be traced to something in our past that blocks us from accepting God's help with a particular problem. This filter from the past that blocks us and causes our distrust generally starts with our original higher powers . . . our parents.

This assertion does not necessarily mean that our parents did anything wrong. In my case, this fact is quite obvious and easy to identify, but that is not always the case. Parents do their best to raise their children, but they cannot control how the child perceives and processes certain events.

One of the most telling examples was that of a close friend of mine. As a little boy, he separated his shoulder and his father rushed him to the hospital. As he lay on the hospital bed in terrible pain, with his dad at one side and the doctor on the other, his father tried to calm him. His dad asked that my friend look at him, and he promised no one was going to do anything to hurt him. After his father reassured him and convinced him to relax, the doctor yanked on the shoulder to put it back in place.

Needless to say, the pain was excruciating, like nothing he had ever felt before. As he stared at his father in agony, my friend's only thought was of how his father had just promised him that this wouldn't hurt. He trusted his dad to protect him, and then he was suddenly hit with the most intense physical pain that he had ever known. From that point forward, he decided that he could never trust his father again, that it was up to him to protect himself. All other experiences with his father that followed were filtered through this experience, and that distrust was carried over into other areas of his life.

There are many things at a very early age that teach us about trust, especially as it relates to a higher power. Initially, our parents and caretakers are our "trust teachers", but they also become a filter though which we experience God. When we view *trust* through this distorted prism of the past, it is extremely hard for us even to consider relying on a higher power for daily direction and guidance in our lives.

Every spiritual book I have read that is worth its salt, including the Bible, speaks of this relationship. In fact, it is promised to us. For me to deny that God is in control of everything requires me to dismiss all these works as fiction.

There is no other way around it. Either it is true, or it isn't.

Try to seriously think about what the world might look like if God were *not* in complete control. This thought might suggest that we were created by a higher power, as was the world, the universe, infinity and eternity, but that we live without purpose, "exchanging our money, buttons and rocks" as if there is no other purpose. That would mean that God created all things, *but is not a detail guy*. He simply started creating and after all that planning introduced luck and chance then walked away. No, that concept didn't work for me. I believe that God is all about detail.

Then there are those who question this "faith business" altogether. There was a group of us guys who met one night to share our experiences with each other, and faith in NO God became the topic. The question was that if all this was created in a vacuum and was headed nowhere from nowhere with no purpose, how did love get in there? If not God, "Oops" was the only explanation that we could come up with, and that sounded pretty farfetched.

If this relationship does exist, which it does, then how do I come to experience it and to know it? This is the truth that this exercise is designed to reveal to us. It is through this practice that we begin to learn the truth and to experience an intimate relationship with our creator.

Hell was simply a place that I created for myself by hiding these secrets about the past—secrets that appear to harmful, but that hold only the power I choose to give them. Exposing these secrets to the light opens the door to healing. Once the secrets are exposed, these experiences can no longer block me from being what our creator created me to be, but I needed to get all of them.

Some of my secrets go back further than I can remember, possibly for generations.

Chapter 15

I am No Longer My Family's Secrets

No one can escape from illusions unless he looks at
them, for *not* looking is the way they are *protected.*
—*A Course In Miracles*

Children are far more observant than we give them credit for.
It is easy for us to recognize their incredible ability to overhear
us when we are whispering something about them. We even
notice their uncanny ability to know when we are trying to
keep a secret about something with which we hope to surprise
them. But when it comes to dark secrets, especially about our
family and our past, we suddenly seem to deny that they have
this ability. We think that by hiding bad things from our
children we are protecting them. This is not true.

In fact, we are a product of all of our parents' secrets, as
they are a product of their parents' secrets. Without realizing it,
these secrets are passed from generation, to generation and the
errors that accompany them are repeated over and over again.
It is only when we look at these truths about ourselves and our
families that we begin to see the pattern. If we are willing to do
the work, this awareness shines a light on why we do certain
things and allows us to break free from these behaviors. The
hard part is seeing them because the victims almost always
protect the victimizer's secrets. It is especially true that a child
protects his or her parents' secrets.

Many people automatically defend their parents, saying "I
had a perfect upbringing, and my parents gave me everything

that I needed." Often, people do not give a second thought to disturbing childhood memories that are still emotionally charged. Recalling these events does not mean that we had bad parents or that they intended to harm us, but because we think they do, we protect them. This fear often keeps us from taking a serious look at the very things that are causing us so much suffering and discomfort as an adult. We are afraid if we look or talk about these things, then we are being bad children or disloyal to our parents. In fact, the opposite is true.

The last thing in the world that I want to do is to harm my daughter, but I am far from being a perfect parent. Sometimes I have no idea whether I am doing the right thing or not, but I do the best that I can. My intent is always to help. I want to improve her life's experience so that she can lead a truly happy and full life. This being the case, I don't want my kid keeping secrets that poison her in an effort to protect me. That makes no sense, yet we do it all the time. I often tell my daughter that I don't always get it right and ask her to understand that her mom and I do the best we can. We encourage her to talk to us about anything that she may question or be confused about, especially as it relates to her feelings and our relationship.

These concerns are appropriately called "family of origin" issues, and many in the behavioral treatment field know a lot more about this than I do. There is a great deal of information to help us better understand these behaviors, but for me, everything again comes back to personal experience. We all have a lot of that.

I have often said that I feel blessed to have had the experience that I had with my family. We are more likely to take a look at these things when they are as obvious as they were in my case, but it's still not easy or even a foregone conclusion that we will look. It took me many years and a lot more pain to become willing to look closely at my parents. For years I said that my mom was a great mom without questioning the validity of that statement. It was simply what I was sup-posed to say about my mom. After all, she had a really tough life. I wasn't going to be so insensitive as to call into question how she performed as a mother.

Even now, it is extremely difficult to tell the truth about my mother without feeling that I am doing something wrong. I want her to be the perfect mom, just as she wanted to be. She couldn't live with her own inadequacies and fears as a mom and she tried to hide them from me. Still, I knew they were there. I also knew that these inadequacies were not something that we talked about because we just didn't go there, so I was already being taught to bury it, as many of us were at an early age. I was taught by my parent's behavior to pretend like the problem wasn't there. That never worked when I thought there was a monster in the closet. It doesn't work on scary secrets either. I can pretend they aren't there and try to convince myself that there is no threat, but deep down the fear remains. Everything I do as it relates to this experience is now motivated by fear, effectively altering the way I approach certain situations in life.

As an adult, I felt that if I said that she was anything less than a great mom, her memory would be tarnished. And that's just it. It is her memory that I am worried about now. It's a memory that I changed, convincing myself that I was protecting her from something. It is this memory that has become the secret that I keep from myself. Ironically, as long as I do this, I am unable to see the truth about me.

All of this confusion and I've been discussing the example of one parent. For many of us, we have a family full of secrets. The most frightening aspect of all of this, at least to me, is that we are extremely likely to repeat the exact behavior of our parents that we are hiding from our selves. So is it really a secret, or is it something more?

When I first came into recovery I still had a successful business. My entire identity was wrapped up in how I thought that I had overcome my family upbringing to become financially independent. This is what had driven me for many years. I believed at the time that this, in fact, was what had set me free from my past. I had no idea what was about to happen to me.

Around the time that I recovered the memories of my father and the murders, I also set out to grow my business. Or so I thought. A more accurate description might be that I set out to explode my business. I thought my business would explode in big way with this new concept that I had created, turning my small local travel company into a worldwide provider of group travel services. It turned out to be a more literal interpretation of the word *explode*.

I enjoyed creating new solutions and solving problems, and I set out to transform the group travel industry. I began to take incredible risks. I was willing to use everything I owned to accomplish this goal and did just that. I believed at the time that I was doing it for everyone else. My goal was to make my family and everyone who worked for me rich. That is what I believed that I was doing.

In order to do this, I started spending money well beyond my limited resources and I was in a hurry. I was certain that I was doing the right thing. I was so sure that I did things before seeking the counsel of others so that they couldn't discourage me. Once I was committed financially, I would then seek out input from people that had experience with growing a business. Basically, I left them no room other than to offer their experience from where I was . . . and that was already committed with all my chips on the table. I paid very little attention to my existing business. In fact, it was if I was running from it as though it were some kind of curse.

All of these business moves were being done at the same time that I was dealing with my past, recording my father on Death Row, seeing his vile threats, the fear of an upcoming murder trial, local media coverage, the family response to all of this and a host of other peripheral issues that accompanied the swirl of confusion. Most importantly, I was dealing with early recovery from my drug addiction and trying to make things right with my family. There was a reason why I was in a hurry and didn't want anyone to question my judgment. It would be fairly obvious to anyone that had all the facts that this might not be the right time to take this project on, but I went for it anyway. All the while, I was justifying it as the way I would make things right with my family.

This particular venture didn't turn out so well. It lasted for several years, but ultimately it ended in financial disaster with the loss of everything that we owned. I was making all this spiritual progress and experiencing all kinds of miracles in my life, but at the same time my ability to make a living for my beautiful family was unraveling. It made very little sense to me, and I wound up back in an old familiar place yet again—hopelessness.

The added pressure of this business disappointment was almost unbearable for me and my family at times. We became discouraged, fought and wondered why this was all happening to us. Hadn't we been through enough? Why this?

That *why this* question is the one that used to baffle me the most. I would let that rattle around my mind in an endless circle of torture, trying to figure it all out. I usually ended up blaming God for it all. Yes, it was my ego, blaming God again for what *it* had done to me.

The difference with this crisis and the others was that I now knew the truth about God and was surrounded by friends and fellowship that I trusted. Aware of the shame associated with this experience, I quickly recognized that I had some work to do on my past to get free from this. This problem would again challenge everything I thought I knew about myself and I would be forced to go even deeper into my family history to find the reasons for it.

The most obvious explanation to my dilemma was my relationship with my father in terms of money. That was easy to see that I had done some awful things with my father for money. I also recognized that he used money in place of love and the lack of it as punishment. To please my stepmother, when I was a young boy, he would give me money to send me away from home for the summer, basically buying me off to appease her. It was his love of money that he eventually killed for. That experience alone was enough to radically alter my understanding of money, and now the added pressures of the business was bringing it all back to the surface. There was some "heavy stuff" in my past related to my relationships with family and lack of money.

I had experienced poverty before. My first memory of it was when my father was initially sent to prison. His incarceration slammed me into a world of lack that I didn't even know existed. I was stuck, feeling hopeless and struggling to make a living. The situation was devastating, and I remember that same feeling of shame. It lasted for years.

I continued to go back further and realized for the first time that my mother lived that way, too. My father didn't give her anything and when I would visit her, he made a point not to give me money. He intended for me to relate that kind of suffering to her, I am sure. She struggled with rent, food and her basic needs. I began to recognize the same feelings that I had experienced with my current situation, and that was extremely helpful.

If there is one thing that I have learned with absolute certainty, it's that I am unable to see the whole picture in my mind. There the picture remains fragmented, and I can see only glimpses and pieces of it. An important step at this point in the process for me was putting everything on paper so I could see the whole picture. After doing the work and then spending time reflecting on it, I was struck with another revelation.

My father was always telling me how the next big deal was just around the corner, about to happen. He told me this when I was a kid, but the mantra really became the focal point of our relationship when I became a young adult. It was the land deal, the pot farm, the property in the Keys, the drug money . . . it was always something. He was always so close and the promise was complete freedom from all of our troubles. When the deal happened, it was going to solve everything. "The big deal" was a promise that I spent my entire life waiting for. It was always just out of reach.

As I reviewed my behavior over the years, I came to recognize that this pattern was exactly how I approached money, and I was still doing it. It was always about that next big payoff right in front of me, just out of reach. Every successful thing I did seemed to fall short of this dream, and I would go again with even greater risk.

In early recovery, I simply transferred this understanding of my relationship with my dad to God. I would do my part to the best of my ability, only to be let down by my father over and over again. This is how I expected God to answer my prayers and when the results continued to fall short, that same feeling of discouragement and hopelessness would come over me. Well, maybe the feeling was not exactly the same. This feeling was worse because I believed that I must be doing something wrong that is preventing me from receiving God's promises.

I *was* doing something wrong and repeating it over and over again in my approach to how to make a living. That old belief system was preventing me from accepting good things because the only pattern I knew was disappointment. I was attracting the same outcome to myself over and over again.

This was an amazing breakthrough, because I never really believed that there was a connection. Like most people, I would probably have dismissed it as crazy if I were reading my own story some six to ten years ago. Denial is how we protect our secrets because then we don't have to take a closer look at ourselves. We mistakenly convince ourselves that it is easier to dismiss this process as crazy, than it is to believe that all of our problems are manifested due to spiritual blockers, most typically from our family of origin issues. It is *not* the easier, softer way and only prolongs unnecessary suffering.

Reflecting even more, it became very clear to me that I wasn't just dealing with my own mistakes, but a family history of mistakes that contributed to my wrong thinking about moncy. I was repeating family history. Much of it had been kept secret, but not hidden enough to prevent me from repeating it.

Money is another one of those things that most people keep secrets about. Most people don't want to talk about how much money they make, what their financial value is, or even what they pay for things. There is an illusion that our personal value in life comes from this number. We often judge others based on what we see on the outside, while comparing it to our insides. It makes no sense really, but that is the way it is.

It is this illusion that causes us to lie and to keep secrets from others and ourselves, even in our own families. The truth about our insecurities become hidden and are passed on from generation to generation. It sounds so simple, but it is the absolute truth. If you have some major recurring problem in your life, take a serious look at your family and you might be amazed at what you find. A surface look will not be enough, because you will not find it. The troubling truths are always covered up in secrecy and protected with false interpretations to protect the imaginary shame attached to it. Look for shame, and there you will find the secrets.

In my family, money was the measuring stick by which everyone was judged. Nothing else mattered. My granddaddy came from poverty and his financial success as a lawyer and real estate magnate became the bar by which all others were judged. I really don't know enough about my Grandfather to comment on what he left behind when he passed away, but there are many unanswered questions. Most of them are protected with the perfect father description of him.

I know that my grandfather was a great man. He overcame many obstacles and succeeded in many ways that no one in our family had done before. He raised a family and provided everything he could for them. He gave them everything that he thought would make them successful men. The fact that many members of my family have experienced worldly failures and alcoholism, indeed, have not lived up to his image does not mean that he was a poor father. It should not prevent us from discussing the truth, either. My grandfather did the best that he could with what he had, but he was not perfect. I love my family and do not have the right to speak for anyone else; therefore I will leave this discussion there.

All of this was extremely important and contributed to the problem, but it only opened the door to what I think was the real cause or trigger. Although I had these revelations, the problem persisted, and with it, my frustration. Sometimes these things take time and the process resembles the peeling of an onion. We peel back the layers one at a time until we reach the core.

Even after all this work on my past, I still had limited memory of my relationship with my father from after he was arrested for kidnapping and attempted murder until sometime following his conviction and death sentence for the Caruso murder. During that time we spoke on the phone when he would call me collect from jail. After being sent to Death Row he no longer had phone privileges, but I visited him there several times.

I remembered talking to him and being with him during that time, but very little about the details of our conversations. I always thought that is was strange that I blocked that period out, but I didn't feel threatened by it. My mind simply told me that it was *after* all the damage was done by my experience with my father, so it probably wasn't important. This, I have learned, is one of the tricks of the ego.

My ego wants me to believe that the past doesn't matter, all the while using it to keep me prisoner. If there is something I cannot recall from such a traumatic period in my life, chances are it is a secret that I am hiding from myself. I had been seeking the answer to my financial problem, but never considered looking at this particular period even though it was one of the final *dark* periods still missing from my memory of the past.

I found the memories that I was looking for *when I stopped looking for them.* It was during my morning meditation on Christmas morning in 2010 when thoughts of this period of time came back to me. It was odd because I was not searching for anything, only sitting quietly in gratitude for what this day represents to me. My mind drifted to this period of time and I was puzzled as to why I would be thinking about my relationship with my father on this particular day. As I started my meditation I was wholly focused on being grateful for everything I had. I was not giving any thought whatsoever to lack of any kind when I began to think about those conversations.

I have really come to trust meditation and quiet time so I did not resist the memory. I did the opposite, asking in prayer to be shown why I was experiencing this and asked to be guided. There was very little or no emotion, just trust in the process. I still had a heart full of gratitude and was not thrown off by this detour; I just simply went along to see where this memory would lead me.

The revelation came first, and then was followed by memories of conversations that supported what I was recalling. After being arrested, my father began to talk about how much the money that he had given me had helped me. He pointed out in every conversation how this was the reason for my new life in the travel industry and how without his financial help it would not have happened. He presented it as though it was something he was proud of, an accomplishment that made everything else worthwhile. He would say, "Son, at least the money that I gave you helped you turn around your life." He would ask if I agreed and I always said yes, thinking that my dad really cared about me. It seemed important to him that he at least accomplished something good in all this by helping his son better his life. I know that sounds absurd now, but at the time, it did not. I was still living in the shadow of it all. It is easy to see the insanity in someone else's behavior, but not so with our own relationships.

He would really drive home this point and I came to believe that he was right. I also thought he kept making this point because he was trying to cling to something positive in all this. It made me feel good to give him credit for my success in the travel industry, because it seemed to mean so much to him. He then added how damaging it would be to me and my career if anyone knew of my association with him. He wanted to "protect me" he said. This part of the conversation really began to ramp up when they started investigating him for the Caruso murder. He casually mentioned that he would *never* speak of our association together, especially as it related to certain activities. He was referring to the burning of the car.

Over the years, as we continued to communicate, any and all success that I had was attributed to his "help" at that particular point in my life. When I got married and started my business, he proudly said how it was a result of the start he gave me and how I was just a bartender before he came to "my rescue", and I agreed.

As I meditated on this new revelation for a few minutes the connections became crystal clear for me. My father's message was very specific and related my success to this money, but there was another connection that told a much deeper story. He attached this success to keeping his secrets. The two were intertwined in this message. His message was: *What I did helped you succeed and you can only keep it if you keep our little secrets.* There it was again, the mark of the sociopath . . . *You owe me.* It was never about me and my success. His comments were only about protecting himself, as it always had been.

This explained why, when I came forward and told others about the unsolved murders that I got busy getting rid of everything that resulted from his so-called help, including almost losing my family. From the moment I shared this secret with others, I began to lose everything that I thought was attached to it. This all happened at the same time. I subconsciously began to rid myself of my existing business and set out frantically trying to create something new that I did not associate with this hidden behavior. The problem with this was that I didn't understand why I was doing what I was doing. Everything I did was born out of fear. Most notably, fear of something that never really existed. It was all a lie, but until I brought it to the light I could not see the truth about these things.

The day after Christmas more about the why of all this was revealed. As I sat quietly and gratefully with this new revelation, thanking God for showing me the cause of this problem, I asked, "Why now?" in prayer. It still seemed a little strange that this memory would return at Christmas, when I was only feeling gratitude and not searching for anything outside of myself.

The answer came and it was simple, as always. The thought expressed through me from that inner voice deep within was that *it was a gift,* and it was given because I had stopped looking and simply trusted. With this thought also came the correction. My experience has been that every revelation includes, or is followed by, a correction and this was no exception. The thought voice in me quietly and clearly expressed this awareness. *Your father and the money had nothing to do with your success and the good things that you have accomplished in your life. It is My grace and the use of your talents that brought that success upon you. I am always with you.*

The end game of this process is to reveal how I perceive relationships and correct them. It really isn't about the money, because that's just another symptom. It is about how and why I do certain things. This is how and where the liability begins to be converted into an asset. What we perceive as darkness and attack becomes a gift, and is transformed into light as part of our special function and purpose. This is truly a miracle that only comes through faith and perseverance. It is a promise, but we must continue to seek our heavenly Father's help to complete this transformation. This is the experience that we are blessed to pass on to others.

As with everything else, my relationship with my parents and family was the filter through which I viewed God, and money was a big part of that. Money had many warped meanings for me, and all of them were tied up in my relationships with others. I too used money to express love. That is why I was obsessed with making millions for my family and employees. That is why I was able to justify the things I did even when they wound up harming the very people that I was trying to help.

The final piece was in the shame that I felt from not supporting my family. This was the hardest to overcome. I came to recognize that I was comparing what I was doing to my family with how I felt when Dad left us broke to go to prison the first time. As usual, this was a lie. Shame always is a lie. I am not my Dad and my circumstances were entirely different. I was making the right choices to support my family and more importantly, seeking God for help.

As a result of this experience, I have more compassion for how my father must have felt when he lost everything—scared and hopeless. *He made the wrong choice* for his solution to this problem and has paid dearly. I felt moved to write a letter telling him how I could now understand why he made the choices that he made. I have forgiven him for what I thought he did to me.

I have also forgiven myself for this mistake. In the end, I came to understand that I simply had made an error that was based on generations of similar behavior and my experience with my father. I was repeating my family of origin experience. I had to go beyond words to find the truth, and in the truth, myself. Now I can begin to make my amends to those that I have harmed with this behavior. It begins with my family.

God is either everything or he is nothing. There is no in-between. If he is everything, which he is, then all things come from him. If there is something that I need that I am not receiving, it is because of my altered perception of what God does for me, and this blocks me from accepting his help.

I still believe that great events will come to pass for me and my family, but I have to let go of the how and when. That part is not up to me. I am simply to seek his guidance and do the work with passion. Then, I am certain good things will happen to me and countless others. I still have these wonderful visions of what to do with the rest of my life, but I am no longer worried about it. I simply want to be of use to my fellow journeymen, do the work, trust, and leave the outcome to God.

Today I have come to believe that our true heart's desires are given to us from our Creator. If there is something that we deeply desire, and if it is good for us and others, then there is no reason to believe that we will not be given the power to accomplish it. After all, why would God's will for us be anything different? That doesn't make any sense to me.

I am not afraid of the past anymore. I want to remember everything.

Chapter 16

Remembering the Truth about My Father and Me

In order to accept God's help in all areas of my life I must first learn to understand and trust his love. In order to do this I needed to go back through my past with vigorous honesty and look at all of my relationships. When I began this process I simply didn't think that the events in my life could be explained to my satisfaction in this regard.

I buried my past because I did not believe that I could reconcile being the child of a sociopathic serial killer father, an alcoholic mother and an abusive stepmother with being the beloved son of a loving God. My life did not seem compatible with the concept of a loving God. I chose to hide from it. I was concerned there would be proof that a higher power *didn't* exist if I looked too closely. Or worse yet, that he did exist, but was a cruel and punishing God.

The hardest part of this examination was always going to be accepting being born into this environment as a helpless child. How and why would a God of Love place me in this situation from birth? This deeper question was always on my mind, and it was the one question that I most needed to answer. I had been through too much to sweep that one under the carpet. I wanted to understand what evil was, and if God controlled it, because if he did, I wanted to know why evil was made my caretaker from birth. From the beginning of this process, that answer is what I was after. This was the relationship that I most needed to examine. I figured if I could reconcile this, I would find peace.

First came forgiveness of the victimizers. This was easier than I expected, once I had cleaned house. My father was a very sick man, and someone told me something I'll never forget that allowed me to let go of this hurt. "He couldn't give you something that he didn't have." That "something" that he didn't have was "love" and that simple statement helped me to find some compassion for my father. Holding him accountable for something that he could not give me was only poisoning me. The same holds true for my mom and my stepmother. There is incredible freedom in forgiving others, but our egos don't want to forgive.

I have learned a great deal about the ego from books and from the experience of others. For me, the ego is really about wrong thinking and is driven by fear. It took me a long time even to recognize that I had fear. That probably sounds funny to someone reading this book, but I thought I had become a tough guy. I didn't realize that fear was the most dominant characteristic I had. I was always afraid of not getting what I wanted or of losing something I thought I had, and most of my decisions came from this simple, yet complicated perspective. My mind, I learned, was the real enemy. This is where all of my problems were centered, including what I had labeled as evil.

As for evil, when I started this process, I believed evil was something outside of myself that I couldn't control. Given my experience with my father, this made perfect sense to me. Some people were good, and some people were evil. My dad, I thought, was pure evil at its worst. I also believed that we were unprotected from evil attacks, and that these attacks were just part of this world, so to speak.

Sociopaths, I thought, were the worst offenders, and based on my experience with them, that seemed true. Sociopaths operate without remorse or conscious and they harm everyone that comes in their path so that also made sense to me. They were evil, they were real, and they were a threat to me in my everyday life, or so I thought.

I had other sociopaths enter my life and harm me in friendships and business so I began to research this topic in great detail. I believe one of the reasons I had multiple encounters with sociopaths is because I was drawn to them. They exhibit incredibly charming characteristics, similar to my father. My best friend when I was growing up had these characteristics. I was drawn to these characteristics because I was familiar with them. The problem was centered in the mind, within me. It was my wrong-thinking that attracted me to other sociopaths.

The Truth for me today is that all the evil in the world is within me and this is where the battle is fought and won. And it is still a *battle* for me. The great news is that I don't and can't fight this battle alone. This so-called battle is where I learned everything that I know about God. This is where I learned that I had an ally, that I was not alone, that prayer worked and that all evil can be overcome. Peace is not only possible, but promised. I learned through experience and repetition that God would consistently do for me what I could not do for myself. Trust came from doing, not believing.

The Miracle of all this is being able to find true peace while you are standing in the fire. It's easy to say you know God or that you can handle anything life brings, but to do it is a very different thing. How would I really know if I didn't get to enjoy this Truth under extreme external pressure?

It was under this pressure that I really began to see God's work. It was in the *coincidences*, in others and in my heart. I started to feel his presence in me, and that gave me great confidence. As I became more comfortable in this relationship, I also became more honest with myself and with God. As I went through these relationships and listed my resentments something unexpected happened. I finally became willing to admit to myself and to God that he belonged at the very top of my resentment list.

I prefer not to speak for others, but many so-called believers seem to go around praising God while tragedy after tragedy strikes them down. They refuse to question God and act as though he is so almighty that we shouldn't question his motives. They simply accept all this pain and suffering without question. It's like a boy whistling in the dark. Not me. Deep down I want to know.

In fact, if the relationship is that of a father (as explained so beautifully in the Lord's Prayer), then I can relate to it. As a father myself, I want my child to be honest with me, and tell me what she is feeling so that I can comfort her. I don't expect her to accept terrible things that happen to her and not ask me why. I can't imagine her being afraid to question me, simply because I am her higher power. Besides, if God is all powerful, then I think he knows what I am thinking anyway. Why not express myself?

I was becoming very good at this "expression" and would even cuss God at times, but apparently I was still hiding something. Maybe I was unconsciously doing what I just described because I had not yet answered my questions to my satisfaction. I had come to see the good in being born into the family I was now, as an experience to help others overcome similar tragedy, but that was not enough.

One afternoon I was feeling spiritually stuck. I was working from my home office, and nothing seemed to be working for me. I was greatly disturbed, and I knew I needed to do something about that lingering trust issue again. So, it was that blocker that I set out to find.

I stopped everything that I was doing and sat as still as possible. I began to meditate even though I felt very emotional and agitated. I was feeling miserable about myself and my circumstances, but I made a commitment to sit there until this was settled. I asked quite specifically to be shown what it was that was bothering me, and then I waited. I continued to be frustrated for more than twenty minutes, but I renewed my commitment to stay until the cause of this agitation was revealed to me. Then it came.

I started crying uncontrollably like a little boy. The first words out of my mouth were, "Why did you put me there? I didn't want to be there. Why did you do that to me? WHY?" For some reason I got up and walked into the bathroom dressing area, I sat on the tub and was flooded with emotions. I repeated those same questions and sobbed as spit and snot started to spill from my mouth and nose as I spoke out loud, my chest heaving from the crying.

I said firmly, "I didn't want to be there. Why did you do that to me? I didn't want to be there." I was shocked at myself as these words left my mouth. I thought that I had come to terms with this, but obviously I was carrying this hidden resentment towards God. I must have been afraid to ask and call him into question until now. "Seek and you shall find," I believe, is one of the promises.

As I sat with this grief, I felt an overwhelming sense of peace fall over me. This feeling was very comforting and felt really good to get this resentment out. I could feel the presence of God in me and around me, comforting me. I recalled times in the past when I held my daughter in my arms as she cried hysterically after a bad dream. The only thing I needed to do was to comfort her until she settled and calmed down. Suddenly, I noticed that the tension had completely left my body.

I have heard this type of experience compared to purging, and I think that is an appropriate metaphor. I feel as though I am relieving myself of something in my system that is poisonous. At first I feel sick from it, but as happens with purging, I feel incredibly good when the poison is out of my system.

After the crying was over, I sat still for a while and tried to quiet my mind. The feeling I had was one of deep under-standing and peace. The overriding feeling was of gratitude for this prayer being answered. I had asked to know what was blocking me, and I had been given the answer. Cause and effect in prayer are not always this easy to connect, but it was no coincidence that this came out when it did. I felt a "knowing of presence" that comforted me throughout this experience. For now, that was enough, but the true meaning of the experience didn't come until later.

Before I try to explain my understanding of the answer to my question, I want to give some background to my understanding of the Truth. This world is only temporary, and that fact is repeated throughout scripture and in most all spiritual teachings. In fact, most refer to this world as an illusion or dream, and the entire purpose of our existence is to awaken from the dream, and then help others to do the same. This is called a "spiritual awakening" and the experience simply cannot be adequately described in words. It must be experienced to be known. It is conscious contact with a higher power.

This is a very sensitive topic for many. People in general find it extremely difficult to consider this explanation, even though it's in The Book. I am always amazed at how many people will say that they believe in The Bible, but then they are willing to argue against basically everything it says. If you talk about its content as Truth, which it is, people look at you as if you are crazy. Anyway, all of the lessons were beginning to sink in and a much deeper understanding of divine wisdom seemed to be available to me, therefore I continued to seek the Truth in prayer.

One morning I was having a conversation with my wife and she posed a question that led me to the answer that I had been searching for. She asked about children being "victims" and how could I explain something so terrible happening to me when I didn't have a choice. Her suggestion was that an abused child is a victim and has no choice in the matter.

This is an extremely important question that I believe goes right to the heart of the matter. I also believe that most people don't want to look too closely at this question because they *think* they may not like the answer. The thought of a Loving God allowing an innocent child to be abused is not very pleasant to think about.

Whenever I am puzzled by a question of this nature

regarding Our Father, I go to the Bible to find the answer. It does not always come easy, but if I persevere, it will come to me. I will find the answer if I ask with an open mind and willing heart.

In this particular case, *coincidentally*, I had also recently had a conversation with some friends about the incredible learning capacity of an infant. One of my closest friends mentioned how a little child can learn an entire language during the first three years of their life with no formal teaching. This really made me re-think how I viewed children. Literally, their learning capacity is at its peak in the first few years of life and dwarfs that of an adult by comparison. They are taking in an entire world of information at that early age and it isn't until we "take over" the process for them with school that it really slows down. Think about that for a minute. A newborn child is learning at an incredible rate until "we" decide to take over and place limits on what they can learn, at what pace and how long it will take.

As I considered the Miracle of this, it opened my mind to other misperceptions of children, with the most important being a child's conscious contact with our creator. Who am I to make the judgment that the child cannot make this decision at such an early age? When I wrote about my own childhood experience in a previous chapter, it was about remembering coming to the conclusion that I was all alone and separate from the world. Did I have another choice, even as a four year old child? The simple fact that I made a decision suggests that there was another choice available to me.

This led me to other interesting questions. Why are some children miraculously saved from abusive or life-threatening situations forever altering the course of their lives and others not? Is it just blind luck or is there something going on here that we have completely missed? Why do we think that we have the power as adults to make these choices, but children do not? When exactly does "free will" begin? That last question really got my attention.

This idea that children could make this choice with their "free will" began to make sense, but I needed proof so I went to the Bible again to see what Jesus taught us about this and I found what I was looking for. This passage is worth reading more than once before continuing.

> Then they also brought infants to Him that He might touch them: but when the disciples saw it, they rebuked them.
>
> But Jesus called them to him and said, "Let the little children come to Me, and do not forbid them; for of such is the kingdom of God. Assuredly, I say to you, whoever does not receive the kingdom of God as a little child will by no means enter it."
>
> —Luke 18: 15-17

When we look at things in human terms it is hard to imagine that this is possible, but we are not talking about worldly knowledge. Changing old ideas about the world we live in is very difficult. It requires an open mind, willing heart and a desire to see things differently. I am absolutely convinced that anywhere we see pain and suffering there is a lack of faith. Not the surface faith that pretends to trust God, but the deep understanding and knowing that God is everything that leads to complete trust. We are not victims . . . we have a choice.

I believe that this scripture states quite clearly that we do have a choice. This understanding helped me find the forgiveness in my heart that I needed to let go of everything related to my childhood. God did not turn his back on me. He was always there. I simply made the wrong choice. Therefore, I can now forgive God for what I *thought He did to me*.

As for my role in this: I did the best that I could, given the circumstances. Therefore, I forgive myself.

Are all of these so-called difficulties worth it if the end game is the freedom to be joyful and peaceful under any circumstances? Does it matter once we learn that all things are simply here to teach us? If everything in this world is temporary and my spirit is to live for eternity, what do I really stand to lose here? What am I so afraid of?

What we are talking about is permanent Happiness, not the kind that is attached to temporary things. We can accept this at any time, but most of us must learn to trust God first.

Chapter 17

Prayer with a Promise of Miracles

There is a principle which is a bar against all information, which is proof against all arguments and
which cannot fail to keep a man in everlasting ig-
norance—that principle is contempt prior to investigation.
—Herbert Spencer, Alcoholics Anonymous, 1ˢᵗ Ed.

Prayer was always confusing to me. The only value that I
thought prayer could offer was that if I asked for something, I
would get it. If it didn't work that way, then it seemed like a
complete sham. If prayer didn't help us get what we were
asking for, then why do it? I was also told to only pray for
God's will for ourselves. Praying only for God's will also
sounded like a complete fraud, designed to trick us into
accepting any outcome and removing any questions about the
effectiveness of the prayer. It sounded very similar to the blind
faith that seemed to accompany requests for *praise God* without
question.

I'd like to say that I sought the answer to this dilemma,
but I am not so sure. That question is not what I set out
praying for. I believe that these answers came to me naturally
over time, as a result of praying. The more repetition I had
with prayer, the more I came to understand what worked, what
didn't, and more importantly, why.

This was a real breakthrough for me because I really had
no idea how to pray. It is my understanding that each of us

develops our own means of communicating with God. There are many books and techniques for prayer and meditation that can help, but this is where our personal relationship with our higher power really blossoms.

I experimented with techniques that I found in books and acquired simple prayers from different sources, but the real miracle came from recognizing that another teacher was guiding me. All these other tools simply helped to open the channel and remove the blockers that had prevented me from feeling and hearing this inner voice. This is the single most important miracle that I have experienced in this life.

Once we acknowledge the teacher, we develop an intimate relationship with the creator of all things. This point is where I found the truth about my father and me. This is where I found my freedom and learned to rely on a power greater than myself to solve all of my problems. This is where I found the courage to face my fears and conquer them. This is where I found what was never lost.

I am not exactly sure when I started praying seriously, but I think it happened a few months after the pain in my back became unbearable. No treatment was working, and somehow prayer just naturally came to me. There were many people and books that suggested this, but apparently, I needed to run out of options before I became willing to try it.

I began to stretch and meditate on my living room floor in the mornings, trying to relax my mind and body before I had to face the day. The main purpose was to prepare myself to handle the constant pressure from the pain in my lower back. I don't think I started out actually praying, but it came naturally when I made the time for the quieting of my mind. My innermost instinct to speak to a higher power was already there, and I just needed to give it a way to express itself.

As I developed repetition with the practice of prayer, I began to find that this was the only part of my day where I actually felt good and optimistic any more. I was unable at first to carry over this feeling into the chaos of the day, but at least it was a start. The more I practiced it, the better I became at handling the difficulties that each day presented. Some days were better than others, but I was always able to get back there if I dedicated the time to it.

This is where the change in me really began to take place. If the day started spinning out of control, I would find myself looking forward to my quiet time, even if I had to wait until the next morning. It was a relief to know my safe haven was always available to me. It was but a beginning, but it was an indication that I was indeed seeking first the kingdom of heaven.

Once I began to feel the presence of my creator in this way, this quest became as important as breathing to me. I wake every morning around four A.M. and spend as much as an hour in prayer and meditation before leaving the house for a long walk. As soon as my eyes open, I thank God for this day and fill my heart with gratitude. Then I ask the spirit to direct my thinking. This sacred time offers me an opportunity to quiet the voices in my mind and opens me up to receive God's love. I have some simple prayers that ask for God's guidance throughout the day, and I offer myself to be of service to others. By the time I leave my house for my walk, I am able to enjoy completely the beauty of nature, and I feel totally connected to an endless universe. It is with this foundation that I begin my day.

As I go through my day, I continue to pray and to ask for an inspirational or intuitive thought whenever I am agitated or doubtful. I try my best to practice presence so that I may see the opportunities that are placed in front of me throughout the day. At the end of the day, I again sit quietly and review my day with forgiveness, open mindedness and a willingness to make a better tomorrow.

Looking back, my prayer time has been the most important part of my journey to freedom. It is here that I learned to trust God. Before reserving this time, I didn't believe that prayer worked. I tried it, but I almost never received the answer that I was looking for—and that was the problem. I wasn't seeking God's guidance, but was telling him what needed to be done and how to do it. That is what I thought prayer was. Its purpose was to tell the creator of the universe what needed to happen for me and for others to make things right (as if I knew).

The fact of the matter is that I don't know what healing is supposed to look like. Mine looked like a train wreck, but it seemed to have worked. How would I know what others need or how it might affect everyone else around them? My need to know is connected to my need to control, and wanting to know often blocks my ability to receive all things without limits. Understanding this was the beginning of true humility.

The way I prayed revealed everything I needed to know about myself. It may have taken me years to see it, but it was there all along. Mostly, I was praying for my own selfish needs without regard for others. Even when I prayed for others, it was for a specific outcome. I was requesting to be helped rather than offering to be helpful. That is not love. It is selfish and self-centered. It is important to seek God's help, and I cannot live without it, but I don't need to tell him how to do it. If I am doing this, and sometimes I still do it, I am not only limiting God, but I am unknowingly preventing myself from having an open mind, something that is essential to healing. A simple prayer for healing and asking how I might be helpful in it is enough. If I am not willing, honest and open minded, I will probably miss the miracle.

Miracles are not the goal, but the result, of accepting God's will and grace. They are not to be pursued, but to be received, as a result of accepting this guidance with open-mindedness. This is where the "seek first the kingdom" becomes truth, but it is only by following this path that we get to see the results. Miracles are always better and will always materialize if we work for them in this way. It may take longer than we think it should, but good things will happen if we stick with it. This is what people mean by the phrase "things happen in God's time." The wisdom of this message encourages us not to give up before the miracle happens. In our daily lives this means to have patience. I hesitate to use that word because many people misunderstand its true meaning. The patience I am referring to is the steady persistence in a course of action—in spite of difficulties, obstacles and discouragement.

This patience applies to everything in our lives, including materialistic success. Spiritual progress always precedes material success, and if I am to have any real success in my future, I must trust this process first. When this success is realized, it will be pleasurable, but my identity and happiness will not be attached to it. There is nothing wrong with pursuing nice things for ourselves and our families, but to find real happiness, material success must be the result of faith in God, not the reason for it.

Of all the things that I have faced in my life, this lesson was and is the most difficult. Learning to trust that I can, in fact, rely upon God for everything is very challenging for me. Trust does not mean that I am to do nothing, however. In fact, to trust requires more courage than anything that I have ever done, because the opposite is true. Turning my will over to my creator led me to face and conquer my fears, not to hide from them. It also consistently puts me in position to help others in need, and doing nothing is not part of the equation. "Do nothing" is a lie that my ego tells me *so that it doesn't have to do the work*. It is another paradox.

Here is how I look at it today, and I think this applies to all of us. When I wake up in the morning, I have to turn my will over to something. Something is going to guide me and make decisions as the day unfolds. What's it going to be? What are my choices?

There are two choices, as I have come to understand. The first and most likely option is going to be my thinking, especially if I have little or no repetition with prayer and meditation. My thinking is my ego, and my ego believes that it knows what's best for me. It *wants* to be my higher power. Its very survival depends upon it. That is what makes this transformation so very difficult. This is the battle: good vs. evil, faith vs. fear. It is here that we need God's help the most.

The baffling part is that many of us continue to make this choice in spite of the overwhelming evidence that it doesn't work. This choice brings us only misery, despair and self-pity. We may find temporary relief in outside things, but the misery will always return. And if you lose these outside things you will no longer be able to hide from this misery. This is the gift that at first appears to be a curse: the gift of desperation. If you are feeling desperate, may you be as fortunate as I was and simply say, "God, please help me,"—and mean it.

When we ask for God's help, we become willing to accept the possibility that it just might work. That is called hope, and it is real. It is God's gift to all his children, because when we get a glimmer of hope, we are feeling God's very presence. We may try to talk ourselves out of it, but instinctively we know it's true. That's why we pursue it.

That leaves us with only one remaining choice, God. Again, God is either everything, or he is nothing. If he is everything and has all power, then how much does that leave me? The good news is that we don't have to understand this or even completely believe it to make a beginning. A simple willingness with some effort will open the door and allow the spirit to guide you. This simple beginning allows us to experience firsthand how it works. There is no other way other than to try this for ourselves.

For me, I began simply to pray for the truth because I didn't know what it was. I also prayed that God would teach me to want what he wanted for me. I was afraid to go all the way, so I became willing to ease in to it. Maybe that sounds silly, but it was a compromise that seemed to work for me. Then I learned to listen. Quieting my mind in meditation was very challenging, but I asked and received the help that I needed. This is where I began to make real progress. In the beginning, I did all the talking. After a while I came to the realization that God probably knew a lot more about me than I did about him and I decided to try listening. This experience is beyond words, I therefore will not waste any on it. Investigate, pray for guidance, and you will find the answer.

The most important prayer for me, the prayer that taught me everything I needed to know about God and healing, is the Lord's Prayer. There are many books written about its extraordinary healing power—and how complete it is, in that it leaves nothing out. This prayer was given to a bunch of guys who had overcome their own difficulties through faith and who had dedicated their lives to carrying the message and helping others to do the same. They were following this one guy in particular and finally gathered enough courage to ask him how to pray. Jesus' answer and gift to us all was this perfect prayer.

The Lord's Prayer tells us what to ask for and how to live a spiritual life. It teaches us the true meaning of forgiveness and its importance. But what caught my attention was when somebody pointed out the meaning of the first two words of this prayer. In the very beginning it states right up front what our relationship with God is. *"Our Father"* tells me everything I need to know about how God feels about me and what I should expect from him. The stage is set immediately in the first two words of this prayer. If I expect anything less I have misunderstood our relationship and denied myself many blessings. For me prayer was all about getting this straightened out.

My journey began with understanding what my original perception of a father was and why. Then I had to move past that and replace it with the truth, a task made easier by thinking of how I feel about my own child and the unconditional love that I have for her. There is nothing that I would not give her if it would not harm her or others. I would not make her wait for happiness. I would not make her suffer to earn my love. I am my father, just as we are our father. We are his children, made in his image. We only delay his love and blessings by not accepting them.

The entrance way to peace is wide, inviting and open to all who honestly seek it. We need only a beginning. The rest will unfold in ways that you never imagined possible. Great events will come to pass, and things you never thought possible will begin to appear in your life.

After all, Anything is Possible.

Chapter 18

Making Sense of Murder with a Loving God

Everything God Created knows its Creator.
                                    —*A Course In Miracles*

One of the things that I have so disliked about most mainstream religious preachers is that they seem to gloss over the ugly part of life. In many cases, they simply tell us to accept it without explanation. "Praise God" was to be our response to everything and I just couldn't do that without some deeper understanding. I wondered, what about all those nagging questions? How can I possibly praise a God that I don't trust?

What I witnessed was too much to accept with a simple "praise God". When I did go to church with an open mind, I was usually left unsatisfied with the explanations offered there. Occasionally someone who had overcome similar experiences would speak, but most preachers talked about someone else's experience instead of their own. It seemed easy for them to stand there and tell me to praise God when their personal experience lacked the "abused child and serial killer father" piece. I don't want to stereotype because there are many wonderful men of faith to be found in churches, but I didn't meet many of them with this type of experience.

One example of those disappointments was when the preacher would tell the audience to "honor thy father and thy mother," one of the Ten Commandments. Whenever I heard this topic it garnered my full attention, but rarely, if ever, did anyone explain this to my satisfaction. I felt left out, and that angered me. Since no one explained how someone like me might be able to do this, I began to question all of it. *Why would the Bible ask me to do something that I could not possibly do?*

Another question that always bothered me was about the victims of my father's crimes. What about them? How does this all fit in with the definition of a loving God? Could I answer this question in a way that would allow me to trust a higher power that could "allow" murder to happen?

And finally, what about my dad? How does that work, and what is his role in existence? Why did he have to do what he did and suffer as he has? Is he also the child of a loving God?

Of all these questions, the one about the murder victims was the most difficult. I do understand that there are just simply things that we will not understand while in this world, but this shouldn't be one of them. It was that I set out to find the answer to. The question was puzzling at first, but something happened that I never expected. I met three of the victims' families.

First, I want to start with my own experience with the killings because that is the only piece that I can ever really know for certain. *Was I a victim or participant in this?* I used many explanations to justify and accept murder in my mind so that I could stay with my father. I would go to any lengths to have my father accept and love me. He was the only higher power that I had ever known, but our relationship was very similar to drugs. We were engaged in codependency.

The peace I found in my father's love was an illusion and never existed. I spent my whole life chasing that, lowering my morals as I followed it into the gates of hell. My dad gave me money, drugs and his acceptance—things I thought would bring me happiness. I continued to change what I valued to chase this elusive dream, a fantasy that turned out to be a nightmare. As with drugs, my addiction to the illusion got worse and worse as I crossed that invisible line where I would do anything and received nothing but disappointment, regret and shame. How did I deal with the shame? By seeking more of the same.

I knew no other outlet to find this feeling, because I did not know God. I had no other options that I was aware of, and this relationship was literally killing me. This was all I knew, and it was crumbling before me into a state of hopelessness. When I look back at it in this light, I see myself more as a participant. I was there because I really didn't know any better at the time, and I was afraid to try something different.

Looking back, there were many times in my life when I was given opportunities to seek a higher power. There were people and events in my life that my inner voice knew were right, but I chose not to listen. I was more interested in having fun. In carefully reviewing my past, I can now see where I consistently made wrong choices because I thought that I could get away with it. All along, something inside of me was telling me my actions were wrong. It is the sum total of these denials of truth that led me to being there. Does that make me a fool or a bad person? Absolutely not, but it does help me to understand that things didn't have to happen the way that they did.

This is a very powerful lesson for me, one that gives me great comfort. It confirms to me that there is protection from events as these if we are willing to listen and trust that inner voice. For whatever reason, I was not capable of doing that when all this happened.

On the one hand, I can easily forgive myself because I did the best I could at the time—while knowing with absolute certainty that something inside of me was trying to protect me all along. Forgiveness is the key. I was unable to see and to understand this connection until I was ready to forgive myself for my part in all of this.

As for my dad? There are many opinions about sociopaths and their inability to feel anything that resembles a loving God. I have given this much thought and prayed often about it. Through prayer and meditation I have come to an understanding about this that has totally settled this issue for me.

Most experts believe that the sociopath is a hopeless case incapable of feeling love in any way. The common belief is that sociopaths are unable to ever have a spiritual experience of any kind. Some researchers cite as evidence their lack of conscience and remorse, but there were a few other behaviors that my dad exhibited that contradict some of these assumptions. In fact, I witnessed behaviors that suggest to me my dad never stopped seeking spiritual peace, even though he didn't know what it was that he was seeking.

There is one thing that my father loved and that was being outdoors in the woods. Anyone who knew my dad would attest to this fact. As far back as I can remember, this was a dominant characteristic of my father's personality. He simply wanted to be in the woods where he could enjoy the incredible peace he found there. He had a deep appreciation for the beauty of nature. He was never very interested in hunting. It was the experience of being away from all of life's distractions that he spoke of and looked forward to.

The first time that he was sent to prison, he would write about his future plans, and they always included having the freedom to get back to the woods. Even after he was sentenced to Death Row, he would write about one day getting out and retiring to "an old trailer" in the woods. I am certain that much of this was motivated by a desire to get away from human contact, but it is where he wanted to go for that relief that stood out to me.

This may seem like a stretch to some, but I spent many days and nights out in the woods with my father, and what I saw in him was peace. He seemed relieved when he was outdoors, entirely relaxed. It was as though he was a completely different person. It may be my own fantasies, but he was more caring and even loving when we were out there together.

Almost all people have experienced a complete sense of wonder at some point in their lives when awe-inspired by nature. These may be brief moments of complete peace and wonderment, but we have all had them. These are spiritual experiences, whether we realize it or not. They are times when we are completely in the present and acknowledging the beauty of a higher power. It is the truth within us that recognizes the indescribable beauty of all creation. This is what my father was feeling, although he didn't know it. Without realizing what he was feeling, he was constantly pursuing this experience. Everything God created knows its creator whether we recognize it for what it is or not.

We are all looking for this peace. Not realizing what we are seeking, many of us look in the wrong place for it. We often misunderstand the things that we are attracted to and why we are attracted to them. Drug addicts find peace temporarily in drugs and pursue it in to hell. The same holds true for sex, alcohol, money, relationships and virtually anything that mimics this feeling.

Everything that my father did, according to him, was done to get him back to the woods where he could enjoy his free time. This was always his goal and how he planned to spend his time. Given his level of consciousness, it is unlikely that getting to the woods would have been enough for him, but he pursued this God just the same. Is it possible that God was offering him love in these moments, but he chose not to accept it? Similar to me, I believe that his becoming what he became was the sum total of his denial of these opportunities and this truth. The same opportunity for love is offered to every one of God's children. Sad, but true, it didn't have to be that way.

In regards to my father's feelings about the woods, there was one event that may be most telling of all. My father buried *his friend* in the most sacred of places in his life, more than sixty miles from where he killed him. He murdered four people, leaving two of them where they were fatally wounded and dragging a third across a field before *dumping* her at the same location as the other two, where she was exposed to the elements. What was the big difference? Bob Regan was considered his friend, and he took him where he had found the only peace that he had ever known. In his confession, he said that he built a campfire near our old hunting camp and stayed through most of the night after he buried him. This was the only victim that my father buried. Even though he did not understand why, he was moved by something in his past to offer his murdered friend this peaceful resting place.

Even after everything that has happened between us, even his vile threats to me and my family, I am the one responsible for my dad's burial arrangements. There is simply no one else in the family to make plans to bury him and he has to write me about this. He has long since picked the location where he wants to be buried: An old cemetery located deep in the woods. He writes me constantly about wanting to be buried out there under the giant oaks.

Recently, I agreed to execute my father's funeral plan exactly as he requested. It wasn't until after I wrote my father, accepting this responsibility that I fully understood the meaning of this decision *for me.*

During the recovery process, I became friends with a beautiful spiritual woman who also happens to be a licensed clinical social worker with a Ph.D. I was not a client of hers, but she became one of my most important teachers just the same. One morning, while demonstrating a wonderful technique that she uses to help people heal past emotional deficits, she treated me to a miraculous gift that corrected years of misunderstanding about my father. Since it is something that must be experienced to be truly understood I will keep my description of it as brief as possible. Words just simply will not do justice to this type of deep work.

My friend helped me to settle into a calm and comfortable state and then she began asking me some questions about my family. She asked me to select items in the room that might represent them, and then she asked me to place them where I felt most comfortable.

First, we started with my father, I selected an object that

was hard, rough and had no qualities that resembled a person. I then selected items that represented my mother and me as a small child—items that were soft, had character and appeared to be very inviting, almost cuddly. I placed the item for my father across the room from me, and I set *my mother and me* close by my side. As I sat with this scene a while and took it all in, I noticed how far away I had placed the cold symbol of my father. It was on the other side of the room, as far from me as I could place it.

She then asked me if I could begin to imagine my father as a very small child, playing in the room in front of me. She asked me what that might look like. I imagined my father as a small little boy about two years old, wandering around the room and playing. I felt a since of warmth come over me. The tension left my body and I could feel my heart begin to soften. She asked me then to pick out an object that represented this image, and I found something soft and loveable that resembled the image I had chosen for me and my mom.

Finally, my friend asked me to create the perfect family for my father and to place them together somewhere in the room. I took the object that was my mother, found another soft object, and placed them right next to me on the couch with *my father* between the two, but touching. As I looked at this image, she asked me to think about what his life might have been like had he been given everything that he needed. I imagined that for a while, and I felt a sense of deep compassion come over me.

I must say that I have no idea what was lacking in my father's childhood that made him what he became, but I do know this. I can no longer think of my father without the image of the little boy in that room, a little boy who somewhere along the line didn't get what he needed either. The emotional deficiency regarding my father is no longer there because it has been replaced with compassion and under-standing. The process of forgiveness has been completed for me.

As for the meaning of my accepted responsibilities for my father's burial arrangements, the lesson is simple. As a result of this healing process, I was able to open my heart and become willing to help my father. It matters not what he has done, only that I offer him love and peace without any expectation. This is unconditional love. Being able to offer this love to my father, someone who still wants to kill me, gives me a glimpse of how powerful God's love is and how it works. If I can give love in this way, then I must be on the road to accepting the truth about God's love for me as well. That *is* trust.

This "completed forgiveness" has also resolved the conflict with "honor thy father and thy mother," answering this question to my complete satisfaction. After I solved that final murder, I was asked by a friend how this part of the story ends for me. The answer came without hesitation, and it addressed that old nagging question. I told her the story of how this commandment used to bother me, and then I added, "through this process I have come to understand that not only *can I* honor my father, but *I will* and *I Am*." I do this through this book, speaking and with the work that I am doing today. I do this by accepting that my dad and I are forever linked in ways that are far beyond my understanding. I do this by sharing the story of our experience together helping others to overcome similar tragedy in their own lives. In fact, I think that has been the purpose of this experience.

This miracle seems to happen regardless of the difficulty when we become willing to invite God into our lives and learn how to accept his grace. It is the invitation that has the power to turn any liability into one of our greatest assets.

Before I offer my thoughts on the victims and their families, I would like to qualify a few things. First, although I have met some of them, I have no business speaking for them under any circumstances. I speak only from my own experiences and my own understanding of these events. It is not my intention to convince anyone of what I believe, only to share exactly how I was able to come to terms with every bit of this. What I understand comes from my own very limited perspective.

I have met three of the victim's family members and that is a miracle. I would like to write more about the healing aspect of this association, but for now we are still just getting to know each other. All of us are in unchartered territory and I think it's best if we let that happen without interference from me.

The part that I would like to share from these meetings and conversations however, is an observation that explained the unexplainable for me. I was always deeply troubled by the apparent innocence with which each person became a murder victim of my father. This circumstance did not seem to be an acceptable outcome from a loving God that supposedly offers peace to all who seek him.

As I listened to each of the family members describe their experience, I began to notice something that stood out in each of their stories. These conversations were not held together but happened independently over a period of twelve months.

Each described the state of mind of his or her relative before the fatal meeting with my father, and the one similarity was the fear that every one of them had of him. All made a point to emphasize how their relatives felt before meeting my father. It seemed very important that they tell me what they heard them say about my father before meeting him on the day they each disappeared. They all had expressed an "inner voice" or feeling that told them not to go. Each of them was very disturbed by this beforehand, but elected not to listen to that inner voice and went anyway.

This speaks volumes about what does or does not have to happen in our lives. I do not know about other murders, but I do have experience with four. In all cases the victims had serious doubts originating from within themselves, but they chose to ignore them. To me, it is quite clear that something was warning them about my father. They were all afraid of him. Why they didn't listen I am not sure. I do know that fear often stops us from doing wonderful things in our lives. Sometimes it also might lead to decisions that can kill us.

This realization does lead to another question that I have come to terms with, and that is, "W*hy do things have to happen this way?*" One of the definitions of God that I have come to believe is that of unconditional Love. God is Love, and love is not forced. If it is forced, it cannot be love, and it is up to us to choose. Love is a choice, and this IS free will. The story in the Bible about Adam and Eve describes when free will, or the ego, entered into the picture. The gift of free will was given to us because love cannot be anything but a choice. If it were not a choice, it would not be love. God, I believe, is constantly offering us this love even when we are not aware of it.

We spend much of our lives believing that we are separate from all creation. We live in chaos and use our free will to choose self-reliance as a means of sustaining ourselves. This choice causes us to live with an uneasiness that is always there, right under the surface. In some cases, like mine, this leads to other symptoms similar to the illnesses that I had that eventually led to my addiction to drugs. Here is where the gift of desperation entered the picture, allowing me to become willing to look somewhere else for relief. When I was out of options, the only place that came to mind came from within. It came out as a desperate cry asking for God's help. At that very moment the choice was made and the door was opened. The key that unlocked that door was a *willingness* to accept his love and his grace in my life.

This Love is so powerful that eventually we will all be drawn to it. I believe, as do many others, that salvation is virtually guaranteed for all of us. How could it be otherwise? Do you really believe that God could make such mistakes with his children that they could not be saved? I don't. Not after all the miracles that I have been so blessed to experience in my life. But, there is another miracle that is even more telling.

In the history of mankind, Jesus Christ is easily the most important figure ever to appear. No matter how you view him in spiritual terms, this is a point with which there can be no argument. He was also murdered. That is how he died. Expressing our faith in God, while being unforgiving at the same time, creates a problem because Jesus' death was meant to teach us the opposite. In fact, if we look more closely, we might just understand that this event was the most important event that ever took place. Whether you believe that he is the son of God or not, you cannot argue with the far reaching expression of love and forgiveness that the events in Calvary taught all of mankind. The very man who was murdered there prayed for his killers. And what did he ask for them?

> Jesus said, "Father, forgive them, for they do not know what they are doing."
> —Luke 23:34

Is it possible that we can use tragic events in our lives to have a positive impact on the future of mankind—by using them as teaching opportunities to help others as Jesus showed us how to do? Isn't that what His Father did? As far as I can tell, overcoming death and sin was the most important message the day of this event was to teach us. If we get caught up in the crucifixion we are missing the whole point. This day is a celebration of release and resurrection. It is not easy to let go of this pain, but Jesus' murder is an example of exactly how we are to do it and from whom we are to seek help. An entire book, The Bible, was written about this very subject.

As for death in a practical sense, isn't this something that we will all experience at some point anyway? If you have any faith in something beyond this world, then you have already accepted that this life is temporary and only part of the journey. In terms of eternity and infinity it appears to be pretty insignificant in the grand scheme of things. Everything about this world is temporary, still man's ego continues to think that he can control it and manage everything from global temperatures one hundred years from now to preventing natural disasters. Even though we have an undeniable history of unpredictable and unexpected events and a universe that has no end, man's collective ego is still obsessed with controlling what cannot be controlled. We can take care only of what is front of us today, and that we should learn to do. When we do that, the future will take care of itself.

I don't know how this works beyond this life experience, but it appears that we must accept salvation for ourselves to receive it. Many great teachers suggest that we repeat this lesson through another life or until we finally get it. I am not sure if that is consistent with the Bible, but I am not concerned with that today. As long as I am here, it is not possible that I would know more than the one who created me, but I am okay with that. If the lesson is infinite, it may take a while for me to get it.

What does matter to me is this. I know that everyone was created equally; everyone has their soul intact and we are all God's children, worthy of his love. And if everyone is worthy of God's love, then everyone is certainly worthy of mine. There is no such thing as a hopeless human condition. Once we get that straight, miracles will begin to happen all around us.

The most interesting part for me, but perhaps the hardest to explain, is how everything always seems to work out exactly as it's supposed to. All of the events that are happening today appear to have needed everything that led up to them to make it just so. I think that's one of the mysteries of God's power in our lives. My belief is that this happens whenever we decide to invite him in along that path. It is a decision that we can make today. As soon as we make this choice, and begin to pursue the path everything begins to heal at that point. All the pain and suffering that it took to get there seems to have happened in the perfect order. If we can accept this healing process, we will begin to understand that there is no need for unnecessary suffering.

It is by doing these things that we come to know the truth about our creator. It is in the doing that we learn to undo the past that has blocked us from being what we were created for and begin to trust Our Father. We are then able to receive the power needed to accomplish great things, including the discovery of our real purpose in this world.

Chapter 19

Darkness to Light *for Giving*

There is no life without love, and there can be no love
without forgiveness.
—Rachel Payne, Bishop Moore High School Student

For some reason I want to start by saying that "why me" is the
question on everyone's mind when something tragic happens
in their lives, but that's not true. I have been blessed to meet
people who don't see it that way. They have learned through
experience and faith to accept life on life's terms. This is where
one of my most important lessons in faith began.

Trust me when I say that this experience is not something
I overcame on my own. It was other people who experienced
similar pain, who shared their experience, their strength and
their hope unselfishly with me who made the difference in my
life. With that in mind, I now attempt to make sense of why I
would be so blessed to witness this type of pain and suffering
first-hand.

Personally, I've always felt the saying "every cloud has a
silver lining" was a lousy excuse for accepting bad things,
especially when the silver lining part was not very obvious. The
truth for me today is that the dots are not always connected in
a way that I can understand them, and why should they be?
These doubts are not a copout, but a starting point. You see,
once I began to accept that a higher power created all of this, I
could begin to accept that maybe, just maybe, this so-called
God has a little more wisdom than me. I'm currently fifty years

old and my limited experience really doesn't qualify me for the job of criticizing a God that created the universe and everything in it, including galaxies, stars, planets, life and billions of souls. To be perfectly honest, this doesn't always stop me from judging what I think of as mistakes that God is making, but it certainly helps to put my judgment in perspective and now often leads to laughter.

Let's try to put this human question "why me" in a context that makes it not only acceptable, but a miraculous gift of beauty and mystery. What is important right now at this moment? Is it past experiences? The future? Does happiness in my past provide me with anything today that I need? Does a good, healthy upbringing make a difference in how much joy I can have today? Certainly nothing in the future can make me happy right now because the future doesn't exist. The answer for me is that none of these things matter. They are all distractions from the truth that I don't need any of it to be happy right now.

This realization didn't come easy and I needed to take every one of the steps that I took to understand fully the freedom of this truth, not intellectually, but in my heart and soul. Many spiritual books point to this truth and they were all helpful in reinforcing what I was learning from others who had overcome tragedy in their lives.

Here's where part of the gift of all the lessons begins to shine through for me. Most people live their lives not realizing that everything they could ever possibly want is available here, right now. They don't seem to experience the amount of pain that it often takes to seek another way of living. A way of living that is beyond imagination, full of peace, love and contentment.

I was always searching for something outside of myself for happiness, like money, success, possessions and alcohol. All these things are temporary, but my belief was that they would bring me happiness and make me feel good. Even when they did, it was always temporary. This type of happiness is not real.

It is an illusion.

Therefore, if the goal is happiness, and I can get there by another means that is permanent, wouldn't that be the ultimate goal? And if this is the goal, does it matter what it takes to get me there? No, because once there, nothing in the past matters anymore. The startling truth is that I already have everything I need right now, and NOW is all we ever really have anyway.

In those times of pure happiness in your life, are you thinking about any pain and suffering that it took to get you there? Or, are you thinking about how good it feels to overcome the challenges you faced to get there? Does the past even matter when you are in this state? No, you are moved from pain and obstacle to achievement and joy. For me, my experience mirrors this truth, only on a much bigger, more permanent level.

Another example might be those times in my life when I became lost while driving a car. I mean really lost, when I was losing hope of ever finding my way. In these cases, the feeling of finally arriving at my destination was always one of complete relief, peace and happiness, nothing like how I would have felt had I simply driven straight there. I no longer cared about the difficulty; I was simply relieved and happy to be there. The difficulty of the trip actually makes the destination that much more rewarding.

For me, the difficulty in the journey resulted in a happiness that I would never have experienced had I not been through what I went through. Ultimately, when used as a catalyst for spiritual growth, the *lost-ness* becomes a gift, one for which I am extremely grateful. In my experience, *the key* to overcoming tragedy is using it as a catalyst for spiritual growth. This is another common theme among spiritual teachings and I have found many of the happiest people on this planet are people who have overcome fear and incredible tragedy through faith and helping others.

This concept used to sound absurd to me. I don't know how else to put it. It took a lot of pain for me to try something different, finally. I am the kind of guy who needs proof, and I didn't see how I was ever going to have proof that spiritual growth could be found through pain and suffering. The problem was I had no experience with this process, and for me to believe that faith worked, I needed to see it in action. Then I heard someone describe the faith we have in turning on a light switch. If I had never tried this, I might find it hard to believe this would work. *I can't see* the electricity and I certainly don't understand it, but a funny thing happens after I do it a few times. I come to have faith the light will come on when I flip the switch. I still don't understand exactly how it works, but as a result of trying it with some repetition, I have absolute faith that it does. Repetition confirms, and *faith comes naturally*!

My experience with prayer and the development my faith came the same way. It developed first from trying, then from learning from others with similar experiences. Ultimately, a conviction in my beliefs resulted from repetition in prayer and practice that offered proof that it works. You can know this truth only by experiencing it firsthand. It is not something that can simply be understood through words, it must be felt. The only way I know how to feel it is by doing it. This doing is often accomplished with baby steps, but God gave me every-thing I needed *once I began to ask* for guidance and help, another spiritual key.

> "Ask and it will be given to you; seek and you will find; knock and the door will be opened to you.
> "For everyone who asks receives; he who seeks finds; and to him who knocks, the door will be opened."
>
> —Matthew 7:7-8

God always answers, but it's up to us to knock. This door is the gateway to peace, but some of us have to go through hell before we become willing to knock. How much suffering we endure has a lot to with our willingness to accept the possibility that it works, and then try it. It really is that simple. In fact, it's promised to each of us.

So let's move on to the bigger picture with my father. He didn't affect only my life, but he murdered several people and affected countless lives through his crimes over the years. I can't speak for others, but I will explain why it is not only acceptable, but a blessing for me. This is not intended to minimize the grief of others. It is *only my experience* that I share. The difficulty in explaining something of this nature is that it takes forgiveness and acceptance before we can experience the miracle and that is not very often an easy thing to ask of victims and their families. Before I could do those two things I could not begin to see the bigger picture, or even think about it for that matter. It only made me more resentful.

I believe our lives mirror the grand scheme of all living existence. Just as they say we were created in God's image and that we are all one body, I believe healing and spiritual growth happen on an individual level and on a universal level at the same time. Just as our lives develop over time, so does the human condition, always advancing towards enlightenment, oftentimes as a result of pain and suffering. I am unsure of what the end result is, but I imagine it has something to do with most descriptions of heaven and it's pureness in peace and love.

So just like the individual soul, collectively we experience what seem to be tragic events at the time that eventually become an additional testimony for the incredible healing power of love and forgiveness through faith. If we had a bigger view of things we would be able to understand the ever changing and growing aspect of this wonderful process. God is love and God is good. Therefore, all things in the end will benefit, just as we do individually when we overcome difficulties through faith.

All things are here to teach us to trust God, often by removing the very things that are standing in the way of a perfect relationship with him. Every experience, every challenge in our lives, offers the opportunity for a spiritual leap that will result in complete happiness. Every trial comes with the offer of a loving hand from our creator to overcome with his help. It is up to us to accept.

Whatever is happening in our lives at this particular minute is in our lives for this reason. We always have a choice between faith and fear. Once fear is eliminated from our lives, and yes this is possible and does happen, a new awakening takes place. This is the destination that we all seek whether we know it or not because with it comes complete peace and happiness. All of the mistakes in our lives are a result of looking in the wrong place for this peace. The wrong place is any place but to God.

When this process is accomplished, the next step is the same for all who experience it. It happens automatically without any effort whatsoever. We become inspired by a deep desire to help others do the same. All people who reach any sort of real peace through suffering have a God-given desire to pass on their experience and to help others find this same wonderful gift of love and peace. The real miracle of life is experienced in giving love and freeing others from their own self-inflicted suffering.

Once we find the way out, there is no greater joy than that of sharing with others how we found our freedom so they may find theirs. This is the greatest asset that a man can have. To give is the same as to receive. Therefore, in giving unconditionally to our fellows in this way, we experience, witness and feel God's love and healing power over and over again. We can't, however, give away something we don't have. That is why we must first remove the blockers to experience this miracle fully.

All suffering is an opportunity to help us overcome one thing, and that is anything that separates and blocks us from God's love. Although we are all part of this miracle, it is only those who turn to God for help that seem to experience it. Others continue to suffer, not understanding that they have a choice.

My experience was that once I asked God for help and began to pray for the truth and forgiveness, this gift was given to me. The result was an experience that turned darkness and attack into light, love, and purpose, creating an extraordinary net gain that can only be described as a miracle. It took work and steps, but the truth is that all people who seek this help with perseverance receive it. We are all His children with the same promise of peace and love. Truly, that is a wonder.

When I see people suffering on an individual level and not seeking God's help, I am still always at peace, knowing that they are still part of a much greater process of bringing spiritual love and awakening to all of us. I do have compassion for those who suffer, and it is always my heart's desire to help them accept this wonderful gift by sharing my experience with them. But in the end, the outcome is safely in God's hands. I am just incredibly grateful to be aware of the process.

Not only does the end justify the means, the journey adds to the mystery and miracle of the whole process. The question of, *Why me? How could I have been given this terrible experience?*, then becomes, *Why me? How did I get so blessed to be given this wonderful gift that found me when I was lost and delivered me to the most incredible destination imaginable? . . . Peace and love.*

Even more meaningful is how this gift of experience is now used to participate in God's plan, helping others reach this same place of peace and happiness. This is the gift beyond imagination and forgiveness is the key to it all. True forgiveness leads to complete release, as if the past never happened.

I believe that we come to know God, *not* in spite of these difficulties, but because of them. Another one of my favorite sayings is, *"The same waves that swamp the swimmer bring great joy to the surfer."* I want to be a surfer.

If I use my experience with my dad as a measuring stick, I should no longer question circumstances in my life or try to label them as good or bad. Those seventeen months with him looked pretty bad at the time. In fact, that time seemed like the end of the world.

And today? This experience is one of my greatest assets. It is a gift of experience that seems to provide others who are suffering in life with inspiration, hope and a willingness to believe that all things do work out for the better, perhaps even helping them to take a step closer to our creator. I didn't plan that, but *I do want it.*

If you don't yet believe in miracles, imagine this for just a minute. All those evil things that my father did in his life are now helping people who are suffering to find their way to a higher power, a loving power that will help them with all of their problems and bring peace and joy into their lives. My dad . . . *he wanted* to harm people, and now his story is helping people find the very peace that he tried to destroy. He tried to take life and now his story gives it.

The truly amazing part of this spiritual process is that this miracle of transforming darkness to light is not random. It is a choice, has distinct characteristics, and comes with a promise. Our Father has given us something that will never fail us. This gift is often referred to as *The Truth* and it is real. The point of transformation where these Miracles occur can always be traced back to a single moment where everything changes. It is the simplest of steps. This step, the smallest ever taken, and often the most difficult, is the triumphant arc between heaven and hell. Jesus described the requirement for this step by simply saying . . .

Be Not Afraid; Only Believe.

—Mark 5:36

This truth is all about forgiveness and trusting where we are, even when circumstances look bad. What other option do I have, really? Facing my fear is scary, no doubt, but in this case fear moves me closer to God, not away. Maybe some fear does have a purpose. I don't like how it makes me feel anymore. It makes me want to change.

The lesson for me is always to work on the inside first and have faith that the outside will work out. This requires courage and action, too. I have great responsibility in that, but it doesn't include worrying about it. Maybe one day I'll achieve that perfect ideal, but today I am on the journey. I have no experience with long term uninterrupted perfect peace. It comes and goes, but I work for it. Finally, something I want that I know God wants for me too.

Some people seem to have an easy path to a spiritual awakening. They have that "bright light" type experience. Not me. I don't know if it has to do with that fact that I am still clearing away the wreckage from the past or my ego clinging to life, but it is all about endurance. I will not quit pursuing absolute peace because I know it's a promise. I now also know from experience that *Our Father* will help me with every step. This Father keeps his promises.

Writing this book has taught me more about myself than I ever thought possible. It has allowed deep dark secrets to be brought to light, bringing me incredible relief from unnecessary pain. There is often tremendous inner conflict that manifests itself outside of us, reflecting the turmoil within, leading some of the people closest to us to believe that we are crazy, still we keep going. Why? Because we have found much of heaven and we know it's real. Once you have felt it and learn that it's promised to everyone, it becomes the only journey really worth taking.

I have been blessed to meet so many people along the way who have experienced the same things, and they told me that *I was not alone.* I have no doubt that they were placed in my life for this very reason, because I could not do this alone. *You are not alone either.*

Letting go of everything that you think you know is incredibly scary, even in light of all the evidence against our ability to get it right. How can we possibly trust something that we can't see, touch or define? I may not see God as one vision, but I see him in you, in the stars, in the heavens and especially in what is not there. God IS what we cannot see that allows everything else to exist, to have a home. God IS that peaceful silence, that empty space that goes on forever. He's here, all around us, in us. God IS Love and we can feel it, know it.

Everything is connected. We are all in this together. When you feel it, you know IT! This is the miracle. It's that we can actually know Our Father, and feel his gentle and loving hand guiding us from deep within ourselves. We simply need to acknowledge that we are not in control of the universe, invite him to help us, forgive the past and pass this gift on to others. Passing this gift on to others is the easiest part because that *IS* our purpose. We were created *For Giving*.

About the Author

Travis F. Vining is an inspirational and educational Spiritual Teacher who lived the real-life horrors of learning his father was a serial killer. In a search for the Truth, this nightmare became an inspirational journey of faith, hope and miracles.

The former travel executive now speaks to dozens of groups a year, detailing his experience with his father and the spiritual journey that followed, allowing him to turn the liabilities of his childhood and early adult life into one of his greatest assets. He also teaches *A Course In ForGiving* and facilitates intensive healing retreats that focus on family of origin issues.

Now a loving husband and father, he has found forgiveness, love and absolute faith and has devoted his life to helping others overcome these same difficulties. He lives in the Orlando area with his wife and daughter. His website is www.victorythroughpeace.com.

CPSIA information can be obtained at www.ICGtesting.com
Printed in the USA
LVOW091511220612

287276LV00010B/26/P

9 781933 523477